THE
BABY-
FRIENDLY
FAMILY
COOKBOOK

THE
BABY-
FRIENDLY
FAMILY
COOKBOOK

From the smallest to the biggest – healthy
fuss-free recipes the entire family will love

➤―≪

AILEEN COX BLUNDELL

GILL BOOKS

WITHDRAWN FROM STOCK

Gill Books
Hume Avenue
Park West
Dublin 12
www.gillbooks.ie

Gill Books is an imprint of M.H. Gill and Co.

© Aileen Cox Blundell 2019

978 07171 8167 4

Designed by Aileen Cox Blundell
Food photography by Aileen Cox Blundell
Family photography by Conor Blundell
Food styling by Charlotte O'Connell
Copy-edited by Emma Dunne
Indexed by Eileen O'Neill
Printed by L&C Printing Group, Poland

Props
Dunnes Stores: www.dunnesstores.com
Blafre.com

This book is typeset in Charparral Pro.

The paper used in this book comes from the wood pulp of
managed forests. For every tree felled, at least one tree is
planted, thereby renewing natural resources.

All rights reserved.

No part of this publication may be copied, reproduced
or transmitted in any form or by any means, without
written permission of the publishers.

A CIP catalogue record for this book is available from the
British Library.

5 4 3 2 1

WITHDRAWN FROM STOCK

To all the

PARENTS

who have been part of this journey

>———<

This book is dedicated to everyone who ever messaged me, shared one of my recipes or just made the effort to say hello and give me a hug. This incredible adventure would not have been possible without you all in my life. Thank you from the bottom of my heart.

About the
AUTHOR

➤——————➤

Aileen Cox Blundell is a mother of three and is the creative force behind Baby-Led Feeding, the multi-award-winning baby-led weaning food blog, which shares natural and wholesome recipes for babies that the entire family will love.

Aileen's first book, *The Baby-Led Feeding Cookbook*, was a number one success. Now, in her second book, she deals with all of the challenges facing parents on their feeding journeys. Her hope is to get children everywhere eating more vegetables, one child at a time. Her very own food revolution.

Aileen lives in Swords with her husband, Conor, their three foodie children, Jade, Dylan and Oscar, and their puppy, Elvis (who also loves food).

THANKS!

To my amazing foodie children – Jade, Dylan and Oscar. I love you more than all the stars in the sky. Thanks for trying everything and for always being brutal with your honesty.

To my husband Conor – I love our crazy family bubble. You are my rock and I love you. Thanks for keeping me going every single day.

To my incredible mother Assumpta, and to Charlotte, Clare and Moya. Thank you so much for all the help cooking and styling these recipes. You have made a friend for life!

Thanks to the team at Dunnes Stores for providing me with all of the incredible ingredients to make the recipes in this book.

To my gorgeous niece Alanna, who is the biggest foodie I have ever met. I'm your biggest fan and so proud to be your best friend.

To baby Matthew, who has tried so many of my recipes thanks to his amazing mum Orla. I hope you like these recipes just as much!

To beautiful baby Sadie,
I can't wait to give you healthy ice cream!

Thank you to my incredible friends, especially Gillian and Jodie, Laura, Darren, Sarah, Emily, Clair, Katie and Darina. You make me stronger by just knowing you, and most importantly keep me from disappearing into the clouds. My feet are firmly grounded!

Thank you to all the folks at Gill Books, especially Sarah, Teresa, Ellen, Catherine and Paul. Thanks for encouraging me to write another book. I hope you are as proud of it as I am.

Last but not least, thank you so much to everyone who gave me a chance and had a bit of faith in me. You are all so brave!

What's In the Book

CONTENTS

01
INTRODUCTION

24
BREAKFAST

74
LUNCHBOX

114
DINNER

182
ON THE SIDE

218
DIPS & SAUCES

236
SNACKS & TREATS

297
INDEX

Introduction: My Food
REVOLUTION

I started Baby-Led Feeding in 2015 because my mother kind of pushed me into it – and by pushed, I mean encouraged. She felt that the recipes I fed my children would really help other parents and as a mother she could see something great in my passion for healthy food.

I shared my first recipe on Facebook on the last Friday of that September, and by the following morning I had a thousand followers. Pretty unbelievable, right? So I took a deep breath and shared another recipe every day over the weekend, and by Monday morning my page had grown to over 4,000 followers.

Thousands of messages came flooding into my inbox asking for help, and I realised on that wet Monday morning that I had an opportunity to really make a difference in so many lives. I started the site thinking if I could help just one person then it would all be worthwhile. Little did I know that I would end up talking to thousands of parents. It became my very own food revolution, my chance to change, make a difference and really help to encourage children to eat more vegetables and fruit.

The more people I helped, the more I wanted to help. Life has a funny way of making U-turns, and now I couldn't imagine doing anything other than cooking and writing. I'm so lucky that I get to be surrounded by beautiful babies and their families for my job!

Between Facebook and Instagram, I now have over **100,000 followers** and over 60,000 parents come to my site every month to look up recipes, chat about their children's feeding journeys and learn how to turn their little ones into foodies.

The best part of running Baby-Led Feeding is the amazing parents I have met along the journey. Mums whose children have been on the extreme end of fussy are now sharing photos of their children eating broccoli and tagging me! That is a really special feeling – it's priceless – and has made every second of this hard work worth it.

In 2018 I partnered with Irish retailer Dunnes Stores, who have supported me in trying to reach every family by making me their brand ambassador. We have been working together to create recipes that are fun, inexpensive and, most importantly, full of goodness.

I have also been working on my own product called Hidden Heroes, due to hit freezer shelves across Ireland in early 2019. Bringing a product to market is pretty much the hardest thing I have ever done – probably because I believe in it so much.

But the most exciting part of my entire year has been writing this new book, which is all about encouraging healthy eating in your family, making cooking and eating fun and, mostly, sitting together as a family and sharing food. I have written it as a mum who has to contend with the same issues you probably do: working long hours, feeding a family of multiple ages and combating fussy eating. I wanted to write a book that would make parents' lives easier!

Creating little foodies starts at your own kitchen table, and these recipes will hopefully inspire you to cook a little more vegetables and use a little less processed food, and will help you stock up your freezer so you have more time to play with your little ones.

I really hope you love it as much as *The Baby-Led Feeding Cookbook*. Remember to share your creations on babyledfeeding.com social channels and let me know what you think of the recipes. I love seeing what you cook and reading your stories – they keep me going every single day.

Happy cooking, and here's to hundreds of happy family mealtimes!

Lots of love,

Aileen xoxo

P.S. The moral of this story is 'always listen to your mammy'!

did you know...
ALL SUPER HEROES EAT SALAD! FACT!

It All
STARTS
HERE

Over the past three years I have spoken to thousands of families, and the resounding common factor in having 'foodie children' is that the family eat together. I understand that this might not always be possible with working parents and busy schedules, but when you can, it is an amazing thing to incorporate into your family life.

Why Eating as a Family Is
SO IMPORTANT

I firmly believe that the way we eat and teach our children to eat will be carried on for years to come. From eating together as a family, children learn to appreciate good healthy food, the effort it takes to cook it and the enjoyment of switching off from life and participating in good family fun. This will, in turn, be passed onto generations of families – all from this one little thing that might seem trivial at times.

It is just as important for us grown-ups as it is for our children – as a parent, there is something lovely about seeing your entire family together. And our children see the importance in sharing stories and celebrating life with the people who matter. Taking a break from our busy schedules to connect with people is a skill I hope my little ones take with them for life. Here are some ways to add a little fun into family mealtimes.

Eat slow and make the most of it.

I love the entire concept of slow food – to me this isn't food that is just cooked slowly: it's the way it is eaten by the family. No parent wants to see food disappear in less than five minutes after spending time planning, buying ingredients and cooking.

The no-phone zone

As the majority of my business is online and through social media, I sometimes forget to switch off and be present. So last year, we as a family – and by that I mean my husband and children – made a deal that phones were never allowed in our dining or sitting room. It took a while to adjust (especially for me and my teenage daughter), but it's been brilliant. Now, instead of checking messages if we hear our phones vibrate, we sit around chatting about our day.

Tell me about your day

Those words alone can bring us to the brink of laughter or even tears. Some days are great and some days are not so great, but sharing our ups and downs has been a great way to stay in touch with each other. Especially as children get older, they need a space where they know they can talk and be themselves. Dinner time in our house is always that space. Talking and laughing about the things we have gone through and helping each other are a great boost to confidence, and many times we've left the table saying, 'You're right – I can do this after all.'

Zero stress!

This is the hardest one, especially if you have a fussy eater, but try to make the dinner table stress free. Sometimes, the less you show you are bothered about your toddler eating their vegetables the more they will eat! Always eating the same food as your baby or toddler will really make a difference too. When they see you eating asparagus spears, they will want them as well – or at least they will see them as the norm and eventually will try them.

Schedule it in

Sometimes you just have to say, 'Dinner is at 6 p.m., be there!' We have a teenager, a school-going child and a toddler, so I know how hard that can be at times. However, if we plan dinners around sports, play and school pick-ups it is almost always doable.

Yes, we have days where our schedules don't align but we try and that's what counts.

Planning is key

On busy days the only dinners we can eat are either from the 'I Need Dinner Now' section of this book (p. 116) or a leftover dinner that I reheat when I come in the door. Planning for those days on a Sunday is usually key to an easy week of food ahead.

Get the kids involved in cooking

One of the cutest things you will ever see is your three-year-old carrying out the guacamole and announcing to everyone that they made it. Usually followed by 'all by myself!' Oscar is always more than happy to eat everything he has made, just because he was involved in the cooking. I find this is a great way to change eating habits too.

Give everyone dinner jobs

Just as with cooking, if your little ones are involved in setting the table, bringing in the food and helping to clear it all away, they feel more included and it becomes a family event – not just Mum or Dad doing everything and the children's only job is to eat.

Try Themed
DINNERS

For a bit of fun (maybe on a weekend), introduce some themed meals.

For Mexican night, we light some candles and play some Spanish music on Spotify. My little ones like the themes so much that they have started to spot colourful tablecloths when they come shopping with me that they 'must have' for Indian night. It's really cute and a delicious way to spend an evening too.

Cooking For a
VEGETARIAN

In 2017 my 11-year-old son Dylan informed us that he wanted to give up eating meat because of his love for animals. As much as I admired his intentions, it also caused a little worry for us. Cooking vegetarian food is not as simple as giving your child the same meal as everyone else minus the meat.

Ensuring they are taking in the right amount of protein, iron and vitamins each day can be daunting, and the thought of accommodating a choice in meals can be really tough – especially when there are four other mouths to feed.

Like everything in life, where there is a will there is a way, and as a result of my son's choice, cooking has changed a lot for us. But it has been really exciting too!

Protein

(Also known in our house as the Bob the Builder nutrient – needed to build and repair.) Daily protein needs can easily be met using non-meat foods including: dairy produce, eggs, beans, lentils and nuts (just no whole nuts for younger children). Most dishes can be easily turned into vegetarian masterpieces by replacing chicken with beans or beef with a side of lentils. You could even make a mini omelette and add an extra egg white to increase the protein too.

Iron

Iron helps red blood cells bring oxygen around the body, converts blood sugar to energy and is essential for growth and normal brain development. There are two types of iron:

- **Heme iron** – found in meats, easily absorbed by the body

- **Non-heme iron** – found in plant sources like legumes, vegetables and cereals

KNOW YOUR FOOD

Some foods rich in iron are:

- beef, pork, lamb, veal
- chicken, turkey
- fish
- tofu
- beans and other legumes
- eggs

Other sources of iron are:

- legumes – chickpeas, lentils, dried peas and beans
- vegetables – spinach, broccoli, Brussels sprouts, green peas, beans

To help the body absorb even more iron, combine these foods with good sources of vitamin C, such as oranges, tomatoes and red peppers.

Other Considerations

As if the protein and iron weren't enough, you also have to consider things like B12 and calcium and other vitamins, so if you are concerned talk to your GP. They will be able to advise if your child is getting the right nutrients or if they need supplements.

The swaps – meat for plant

Lots of the recipes throughout this book can be adapted to be vegetarian (if they are not already). I have included notes throughout with handy swaps to make your vegetarian meal times that little bit easier.

The Ultimate Guide to
FUSSY EATING

Having a fussy kid is so stressful for parents. I have been there, and I can admit I have gone to another room to have a little cry at times. There is nothing nice about cooking an entire dinner and your little one not eating a single bite.

It happens, and if you are reading this, you are more than likely going through this right now. First, take a deep breath and don't beat yourself up! It can change, regardless of your child's age. Whether you made purées, did baby-led weaning or used a mix of both, children have minds of their own and can one day dislike a food they always previously loved.

When you think about it, food is one of the few things a small child has complete control over. You can't force them to eat or it will just make the situation worse. They own their decision and decide what they choose to swallow. The worst part is that the harder you push, the more they will fight back – and then they win!

Getting your children to eat veggies is a long-term goal, so don't get disheartened if it takes longer than you expect. The aim is to make eating veggies and fruit fun and to really praise their efforts, no matter how tiny they are. Every little bit helps and is a step in the right direction. It will change, sometimes painfully slowly, but it will – I promise!

Tips on creating a veggie- and fruit-loving child

Eat together. If you are eating broccoli and making a big deal about how yummy it is, then your baby or toddler will be more inclined to try it.

Talk about veggies and their benefits, especially when you are eating them. For example: carrots help you to see; peppers help you to grow strong!

Always put veggies on their plate, then encourage them to eat just one little bite. Be really complimentary when they do and ignore the veggies left over. Remember that it's a long-term goal.

Shopping Together. Get your little ones to help choose fruit and veg in the supermarket and then prepare them at home – they love being involved in cooking and it encourages tasting.

Feel my muscles! This is a trick that always worked with Oscar. When he eats his broccoli now, he always asks us to feel his muscles and we make a big deal about how strong they are.

Snack on veggies. Raw veggies are a great snack for older toddlers (though not for smaller babies). Oscar loves to dip and crunch, especially when he is eating carrot or pepper pig sticks (as peppers are called in our house).

Make eating veggies the norm, so your child sees them every day.

NOTE! If your little one is fussy, not looking for or caring about alternatives and losing weight, it is important to speak to a dietician.

What Is
BABY-LED FEEDING

Baby-led feeding (also known as baby-led weaning) is a natural exploration of food. This is encouraged by giving your baby wholesome and naturally delicious foods that they will grab, explore and put into their mouths all by themselves.

How to know when your baby is ready

- Your baby is six months old, able to sit up unsupported and has good neck strength.
- Your baby has lost the reflex to push foods to the front of their mouth.
- Your baby is reaching out and grabbing foods.
- Your baby is chewing, even if they have no teeth.

How to give vegetables and fruit to your baby

When you are giving fruits and vegetables, cut them into thick chip sizes. This makes them easier for small babies to manage, as they can get frustrated if the food is too small to pick up. Just remember that all food should break apart when squashed between your thumb and index finger.

First foods to get you started

Avocado

Banana

Sweet potato

Melon

Beans

Oily fish

Meat (shredded)

Green veg

Eggs (fully cooked - not soft boiled)

Steamed vegetables

Allergies and
SUBSTITUTIONS

When your baby starts weaning, allergies are always a worry – especially when introducing highly allergenic foods like nut butters or eggs. If you or anyone in your family has a reaction to dairy, nuts, shellfish or any other allergen, speak to your healthcare provider prior to introducing these foods to your baby.

Gluten

It is important to introduce your baby to gluten before they are seven months old to minimise the risk of coeliac disease. Gluten is found in bread, pasta and cereals, and there is no reason to not give these foods to your little one unless they have been diagnosed with a gluten intolerance. If there is already a coeliac person in the family, there are some special steps you should take before giving your baby gluten. Coeliac Ireland recommend 'offering small amounts of gluten daily from 6 months so that if the disease does develop a blood test would be conclusive'.

Thankfully none of my children have allergies, and we all eat bread and pasta. However, I like to use buckwheat in my recipes for pancakes, cakes and cookies because it is super-nutritious and yummy – you can always use regular white flour instead if you wish.

Alternatives

If your child has been diagnosed with an allergy, or if you or your family are vegan and don't want to use dairy, there are many alternatives you can use when making my recipes.

Ingredient	Replace with
1 egg	1 tablespoon flaxseed soaked in 3 tablespoons hot water for a few moments **or** 1 tablespoon ground chia seeds in 3 tablespoons of hot water
Cow's milk	Oat milk, organic rice milk
Butter (dairy)	Avocado, nut butters, coconut oil, olive oil
Wheat flour	Buckwheat flour, coconut flour, oat flour
Nuts	Seeds, beans
Yogurt	Vegan yogurt
Gelatine	Agar Agar (available in all good health stores)

SAFETY TIPS

Choking is a really scary thought and one that is at the forefront of our thoughts when we start letting our little babies feed themselves. However, once you only offer soft and safe foods, your baby is quite capable of chewing and breaking up the food with their strong gums.

know the difference between
GAGGING & CHOKING

Gagging

Gagging is a common occurrence in early baby-led feeding, although it might never happen at all. The gag reflex is a safety mechanism that prevents choking while babies learn to move food from the back of their throat to the front. Gagging also teaches them not to stuff their mouth with food. As babies grow older and more skilled at eating, they gag less and chew more.

Choking

Choking is when food moves past the gag reflex and into the airway, causing partial or full obstruction of the airway and allowing no or little oxygen to get to the lungs. Choking is much more serious than gagging and requires immediate intervention. The most commonly choked-on foods for children under five are grapes, cherry tomatoes and nuts. The risk of choking is the same for babies who are purée fed as it is for those who are doing baby-led feeding.

Keeping your baby safe

1. Make sure your baby is ready – they should have reached the milestones described on page 14.

2. Don't put food into your baby's mouth (or let anyone else either). Baby-led feeding is about putting your baby in control of what they eat.

3. Avoid foods that pose a choking threat, including nuts, whole grapes, whole berries, popcorn and hard chunks of fruit or vegetables.

4. Never, ever, **ever** leave your baby alone when eating.

5. Cut small fruits like grapes, blueberries or olives into safe pieces. Grapes should be cut lengthways – I always cut mine into quarters just to be really safe.

6. Make sure the food is soft enough. Does it break up if you squeeze it between your index finger and thumb? If so, then your baby should be able to chew it.

7. Give your little one time to eat – they are small and just learning.

8. When your baby is full they will stop eating. Don't try and force them to eat 'one more spoon'.

9. If your baby does gag, do not stick your own fingers into their mouth or startle them as this could lead to choking.

If you are still worried about what to do if your baby gags or chokes, try a course in infant first aid to put your mind at ease.

Making This Book

WORK
FOR YOU

One of the biggest struggles in the kitchen is cooking lots
of meals for different members of the family and these
variations in dishes or entire recipes can very quickly
become a stressful situation for parents. This is where
you take a huge breath in and breathe out a sigh of relief,
because this book is here to help you and make your time in
the kitchen a much better and more fun experience.

One Meal For the
ENTIRE FAMILY

This book is packed with 150 recipes made by a mum for other mums and dads suitable for all ages – from babies to toddlers, school children to teenagers and mums and dads to grandparents: one meal for the entire family that is healthy, nourishing and also stress free!

I'm not an adventurous cook, and even I don't like spending hours in the kitchen – especially on my days off, when I want to play with my children.

The recipes are simple and easy to follow, but you can experiment a little and put your own spin on them!

Season to your own preference

I don't use salt in any of my recipes as babies don't need added salt in food. It's really easy for grownups to sprinkle a little salt on their food before bringing it to the table.

Add a little more vegetables

As a parent, I find nutritional advice can be very conflicting at times. One day fat is good, then it's bad, then sugar is good and then it's bad. The one thing, however, that remains constant is that we should be eating more vegetables. So add more in where you can and get the kids eating their greens.

Experiment

Maybe you like less garlic or perhaps you like a thicker sauce. Part of the fun of making food is experimenting.

Use a little less sugar

I use maple syrup or Medjool dates as sweeteners throughout my treat recipes. You will find that when you reduce the sugar in your diet, your tastebuds will come to life! Use a little less sweetener every time you make a recipe until you have it at an acceptable level as a treat for you and your family.

Get the kids to help

Because the recipes are so easy, they are great for getting the little ones involved in the cooking process. Toddlers especially love helping, which is so cute! Just put on an apron, bring over a chair for them to stand on and get them mixing and cutting out dough.

A Guide to
SYMBOLS

I want to ensure this book makes your life as easy as possible, so you will find these handy symbols throughout the book to guide you in your everyday cooking adventures. I understand that sometimes you might have a toddler holding onto your legs as you cook dinner, or you might really just want a meal now because your day has been crazy, so these symbols will guide you depending on the time, whether you want to make a double meal or even if you just want a lunchbox filler.

| Freeze Me | BLW Friendly | Vegetarian | Lunchbox | Quick Meal |

Food For FREEZING

I freeze so much food that I am seriously thinking about getting a chest freezer. Well, not quite, but I am a huge advocate for cooking fresh, wholesome food in my kitchen, then freezing it to lock all of that goodness in.

The concept behind *Baby-Friendly Family Food* is that life around food should be easy and meal times should be fun, and, for me, freezing is a huge part of that. There is something so satisfying and easy about reaching into the freezer to grab an entire cooked dinner and know that I have nothing else to do but defrost and reheat.

Besides the convenience of freezing, it also helps to reduce food waste, which is great for the environment and our pockets. No one wants to see good food go in the bin!

Pre-roast veggies and freeze

Cut up butternut squash or sweet potatoes and roast at 180°C until soft and cooked through (about 30 minutes). Allow to cool fully, then place into a freezer bag, label with the date and freeze. These are so handy to have for soups and sauces and save a ton of time.

Freezing in season

Cooking in season is the cheapest way to buy vegetables and fruits. If you have even one free drawer in your freezer, fill it up with freezer bags packed with freshly washed produce. I wash and freeze berries, spinach and kale – perfect for smoothies or muffins.

Double up dinners

Making a double dinner is often just as quick as making one. You have the ingredients on hand and it may be as simple as chopping one more onion or red pepper. Eat one dinner on the day, then allow the rest to cool fully before covering and freezing for when you really need it.

Leabharlann Contae na Mí

Stock up on lunchbox fillers

Lunchboxes are the bane of most parents' lives, so it is really handy to have at least five lunches you know your child will love in the freezer. Smaller bite-sized ones will defrost really quickly, but take larger things like pies out of the freezer the night before. Healthy lunchbox muffins freeze really well and a batch makes 24 – that's a lot of school lunches in just one easy recipe!

Stack it up

To pack even more into your freezer, fill up freezer bags, seal, then lay them flat in the freezer until frozen solid. You can then stack them easily beside each other and fit in much more food.

Bananas galore

You will always find at least four bags of frozen banana in my freezer at any time. Bananas are on offer quite regularly, so buy in bulk, peel, chop, throw into a bag and freeze! They are great for adding to smoothies, recipes like my granola (see page 34) and sweetening pancakes.

YOU DON'T NEED TO COOK SEPARATE MEALS FOR YOUR BABY.

It's really true!

A Bright Start
BREAKFAST

I am one of those mothers who is constantly telling their children how 'a good breakfast will set you up for the day ahead'. But weekdays can be crazy! With both parents working in most homes, and kids at school and crèche, we're all running around like headless chickens, so breakfast has to be seamless.

My teenage daughter likes to grab and go, while my sons like a feast in the mornings – but they also like to take their time. So having food prepared ahead makes breakfast easy and quick.

In this section you will find:

Make-Ahead Breakfasts

10-Minute Wonders

Lazy Weekends

Make-Ahead
BREAKFASTS

Recipes you can make in advance and either freeze or keep in your fridge. Great for grab and go!

OATMEAL
POWER COOKIES

MAKES 12

When the alarm doesn't go off in time and you are in a real rush, these cookies are amazing. Sweetened with just banana and loaded with brain-nourishing linseed, they make a perfect breakfast for busy kids and parents too.

180g (2 cups) oats
70g (1 cup) grated carrot
70g (½ cup) sunflower seeds
70g (½ cup) pumpkin seeds
70g (½ cup) linseeds
1 tsp baking soda
3 bananas, mashed
2 tbsp maple syrup
2 eggs
1 tsp vanilla extract
60g (2oz) good quality raw chocolate, to decorate

Preheat oven to 180°C/350°F/gas 4.

Put all of the ingredients, except the chocolate, into a large bowl and stir well to combine.

Line a baking tray with parchment paper. Use an ice-cream scoop to measure out 12 cookies, then press each cookie down a little with a fork into a thick cookie shape.

Bake for 15 minutes until golden brown, then remove from the oven and cool on a wire rack.

Melt the chocolate and drizzle over the cooled cookies.

Store in an airtight container.

Overnight oats are one of the most popular recipes from my first book, so I wanted to give you some more variations. Overnight oats are perfect for kids of all ages and ideal for those busy mornings when you need something nourishing on the go.

APPLE PIE
OVERNIGHT OATS

SERVES 1 ADULT & 1 CHILD

Delicious caramelised apples, combined with cinnamon and a whole lotta love!

1 banana
90g (1 cup) oats
250ml (1 cup) milk of your choice
1 tbsp flaxseed
¼ tsp cinnamon
¼ tsp nutmeg
¼ tsp ground ginger

For the caramelised apples
(enough for 3 jars)
1 tbsp maple syrup
1 tbsp rapeseed or coconut oil
½ tsp cinnamon
3 sweet eating apples, peeled
and roughly chopped

Mash the banana then add to a jar along with the oats, milk, flaxseed and spices. Give it a really good stir, then leave aside.

Place the maple syrup, oil and cinnamon in a saucepan and stir over a medium heat until it starts to caramelise – it should turn a deep golden colour and begin to thicken.

Add the apple and stir to coat really well. Heat gently until the apple starts to soften then take off the heat and leave to cool fully.

Place a layer of apple on top of the oats (keep any leftovers in a sealed jar), then leave in the fridge overnight.

Serve warm or cold.

AILEEN'S TIP!
Overnight Oats can be served both warm or cold. To heat, empty into a microwaveable bowl and heat for about 30 seconds, until warmed through.

PEANUT BUTTER & JAM
OVERNIGHT OATS

SERVES 1 ADULT & 1 CHILD

This is a recipe kids really love – the bowls are always licked clean!

90g (1 cup) oats
250ml (1 cup) milk of your choice
1 heaped tbsp peanut butter,
plus 1 tsp for topping
1 tsp maple syrup
2 heaped tbsp blackberry jam
(see page 234), plus 1 tsp for
topping

Add the oats, milk, peanut butter and maple syrup to a bowl and mix until smooth and creamy.

To a jar, add the 2 tbsp blackberry jam, then carefully spoon the oat mixture over it.

Top with the extra peanut butter and jam.

Sprinkle with a few oats then leave in the fridge overnight.

Serve warm or cold.

CHOCOLATE SPREAD & BANANA
OVERNIGHT OATS

SERVES 1 ADULT AND 1 CHILD
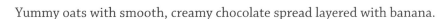

Yummy oats with smooth, creamy chocolate spread layered with banana.

1 tbsp Notella (see page 232)
90g (1 cup) oats
250ml milk (1 cup) of your choice
1 banana, ½ mashed and ½ sliced
crushed hazelnuts, to decorate

Start by drizzling a little Notella around the inside of the jar to decorate.

Add the oats, milk and mashed banana to a bowl and stir well.

Spoon a third of the oat mixture into the jar, then drizzle over some more Notella, a third of the sliced banana and repeat until all the ingredients are used up.

Sprinkle the crushed hazelnuts on top to decorate, then leave in the fridge overnight.

Serve warm or cold.

EASY-PEASY
RHUBARB OAT BAKE

MAKES 24 SQUARES

This is such a simple recipe and it's packed with goodness. The best thing is that you can cook it ahead, then portion it into squares and freeze. You can also switch up the fruit if you are not a fan of rhubarb.

270g (3 cups) oats
120g (1 cup) buckwheat flour
1 tsp baking powder
40g (½ cup) desiccated coconut
120g (¾ cup) coconut oil, melted
2 bananas, mashed
4 tbsp maple syrup
1 egg
1 tsp vanilla extract
5 rhubarb stems, cut into small chunks
2 oranges, juice only
1 tbsp maple syrup
1 tbsp chia seeds

Preheat oven to 180°C/350°F/gas 4.

Add the oats, flour, baking powder and 30g of the desiccated coconut to a bowl. Give it a good stir, then make a well in the middle and add the coconut oil, bananas, 3 tbsp of the maple syrup, the egg and vanilla. Stir until it's fully combined and has formed a dough.

Line a 25 x 25cm tin with parchment paper, then pour in three-quarters of the mixture, press it down with a spoon and leave aside.

Place the rhubarb in a saucepan with the orange juice. Bring to the boil, then turn the heat to low and mash using a wooden spoon or masher. Then add 1 tbsp of the maple syrup and the chia seeds and give it a good stir.

Pour the rhubarb mixture over the oats, then dollop over the remaining oat mixture.

Sprinkle the remaining desiccated coconut on top and bake for 15 minutes.

Cool fully before removing from the tray, then slice into squares and serve.

NUT & SUGAR-FREE
FRUIT GRANOLA

MAKES 1 LARGE JAR

Granola is quick, full of goodness and inexpensive to make. I love having this in the cupboard ready to go for busy days. Just sprinkle over Greek yogurt, add a few berries and you have one of the loveliest treats ever!

360g (4 cups) oats
80g (1 cup) desiccated coconut
70g (½ cup) sunflower seeds
35g (¼ cup) linseeds
35g (¼ cup) pumpkin seeds
2 tsp ground cinnamon
4 tbsp rapeseed oil
4 tbsp coconut oil
3 bananas

Preheat oven to 160°C/325°F/gas 3.

Add the dry ingredients to a bowl and stir well.

Pour the oils into a blender, add the banana and blend until smooth and creamy. Then pour into the oat mixture and stir well.

Line a baking tray with greaseproof paper, add the granola and spread out evenly.

Cook for around 15 minutes, then remove and toss with a spatula. Cook for a further 10–15 minutes until golden brown.

Cool fully before serving.

AILEEN'S TIP!
To serve granola to small babies or toddlers simply grind the seeds before adding to yogurt or fruit.

RASPBERRY PORRIDGE
MINI MUFFINS

MAKES 24

The number one recipe on the Baby-Led Feeding website is definitely my breakfast muffins – mainly because they are a great way of getting little ones to eat porridge without the mess.

180g (1¾ cups) wholemeal flour

100g (1 cup) porridge oats

1 tsp baking powder

1 tsp baking soda

1 lemon, zest and juice

50g (⅓ cup) sunflower seeds, ground

150ml (¾ cup) stewed sweet apples

125ml (½ cup) Greek yogurt

1 egg

60ml (¼ cup) rapeseed oil

1 tsp vanilla extract

125g (1 cup) raspberries

Preheat oven to 180°C/350°F/gas 4.

Add the flour, porridge oats, baking powder, baking soda, lemon zest and sunflower seeds to a large mixing bowl.

In a jug, whisk the stewed apples, Greek yogurt, egg, oil and vanilla until well combined.

Make a well in the centre of the flour and oat mixture and slowly whisk in the wet mixture until it forms a smooth batter, then fold in the raspberries.

Spoon the mixture into a lightly oiled mini-muffin tin then bake for 20 minutes until the muffins have risen and are golden brown – if you stick a toothpick into them it should come out clean.

Remove from the tin and serve warm or cold. They keep in an airtight container for up to a week, or you can freeze them for handy breakfasts on the go.

AILEEN'S TIP!

These muffins defrost super quickly! Thow one in your baby bag for those days you are out and about and your baby needs a healthy snack.

KID-HAPPY
CHIA PUDDING

SERVES 1 ADULT & 1 CHILD

Creamy, filling and my kids think it tastes like dessert for breakfast. This recipe is so easy that my four-year-old can make his own! The rules are: one portion each of fruit, chia seeds and milk. Simple.

85g (½ cup) chia seeds

375ml (1½ cups) milk of your choice

40g (¼ cup) fresh pineapple, puréed

juice ½ lemon

¼ tsp ground ginger

3 heaped tbsp Greek yogurt

sliced pineapple, to serve

1 tsp desiccated coconut, to decorate

Place the chia seeds, milk, pineapple purée, lemon juice and ginger into a bowl and stir well. Cover, then refrigerate overnight.

The next morning divide the mixture between 3 serving glasses, and top each one with a heaped tablespoon of Greek yogurt and a little pineapple.

Sprinkle over a little desiccated coconut and serve.

BEAN AND NUT
BREAKFAST BARS

MAKES 12

Beans are really high in protein and are nourishing too, so they make an ideal breakfast. You don't normally associate beans with breakfast bars but, honestly, these work and they taste really delicious too.

400g tinned black beans, drained

135g (1½ cups) oats

2 tbsp rapeseed oil

3 tbsp maple syrup

1 tsp vanilla extract

70g (½ cup) pumpkin seeds (grind for babies without teeth)

70g (½ cup) sunflower seeds (grind for babies without teeth)

1 egg

140g (½ cup) smooth peanut butter

60g (2oz) good quality raw chocolate, melted, to decorate

Preheat the oven to 180°C/350°F/gas 4.

Add the beans to a large bowl and use a masher to break them up.

Place all the other ingredients, except the chocolate, into the bowl and mix well.

Pour into a 26 x 20cm tin lined with greaseproof paper and press down with a spoon.

Bake for 25 minutes until golden brown.

Allow to cool fully then pour the melted chocolate over. Leave to set fully before cutting into bars and serving.

Store in an airtight container for 1 week.

AILEEN'S TIP!
Make the apple compote ahead of time and freeze in a large ice cube tray. Just defrost them when you are ready to make the jars.

APPLE CRUMBLE
PARFAIT

SERVES 2 ADULTS & 2 CHILDREN

The prettiest and tastiest breakfast you will probably ever make – and the easiest too. I prepare the crumble ahead of time to make it even quicker! Make the night before so you wake up to these yummy jars in your fridge.

For the spiced apple compote
3 sweet eating apples, cored and cut into chunks
1 orange, zest and juice
1 tbsp grated ginger
½ tsp cinnamon
½ tsp nutmeg

For the crumble
30g (¼ cup) pumpkin seeds
30g (¼ cup) sunflower seeds
3 Medjool dates
2 tbsp olive oil
90g (1 cup) oats
½ tsp cinnamon
½ tsp nutmeg

For the yogurt cream
200g (1 cup) Greek or natural yogurt
1 large banana, mashed

Preheat the oven to 180°C/350°F/gas 4.

To make the compote, place the apple chunks in a saucepan with the juice of the orange (leave the zest aside for the crumble), grated ginger, cinnamon and nutmeg.

Bring to the boil then reduce the heat to its lowest setting, cover the pot with a lid and simmer for 5–6 minutes, until the apple is soft. Take off the heat and allow to cool fully.

To make the crumble, first pour the seeds onto a tray and place in the oven for about 10 minutes, until they start to turn golden.

Add the seeds to a food processor and process until broken up. Then add the Medjool dates and oil and blend until it forms a paste.

Pour into a bowl, add the oats, orange zest and spices and, using your hands, work into a crumble mixture.

Turn onto a baking sheet lined with parchment paper and bake for 10–12 minutes, until the mixture is golden in colour. Then remove from the oven and leave to cool.

To make the yogurt topping, add the yogurt to a bowl and stir in the banana until it forms a smooth, creamy sauce.

To assemble your jars, first add a few tablespoons of the apple compote, then a layer of the crumble, before topping with yogurt.

To decorate, sprinkle a little more crumble on top.

BREAKFAST FRITTATA
MINI MUFFINS

MAKES 24

One of the easiest, quickest breakfasts you can make and the kids love them.
I load them with vegetables that are chopped up super small, which really works,
as they can't pick them out! You can make these ahead and freeze them –
they defrost quickly and heat up in the microwave.

2 tbsp rapeseed oil
1 red pepper, finely diced
1 medium onion, finely diced
2 cloves garlic, crushed
2 large handfuls fresh baby leaf spinach, roughly chopped
12 basil leaves, roughly chopped
6 eggs
black pepper, to season
50g (¼ cup) Cheddar cheese, grated

Preheat oven to 180°C/350°F/gas 4.

Heat the rapeseed oil in a frying pan over a medium heat, then gently fry the pepper and onion until soft. Add the garlic and cook for a further 3 minutes.

Remove the pan from the heat and add the spinach and basil. Stir well. The leaves should wilt slightly with the heat from the onions and peppers.

In a bowl, whisk the eggs and season with a little pepper. Pour this over the vegetable mixture, add the cheese and stir well.

Spoon into a mini-muffin tin and bake in the oven for 12 minutes, until the egg mixture puffs and is set through.

Remove the frittatas from the tin and cool before serving.

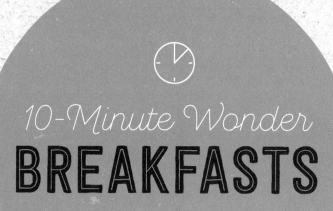

10-Minute Wonder
BREAKFASTS

Recipes you can make in advance and
either freeze or keep in your fridge.
Great for grab and go!

Mammy's Yummy
PORRIDGE

This is Oscar's absolute favourite breakfast. Since he was a baby, we have eaten this up to three times a week in all sorts of combinations. Daddy does try to make it but, according to Oscar, it's called Mammy's Yummy Porridge because only Mammy can make it right.

MAMMY'S YUMMY PORRIDGE

SERVES 1 ADULT & 1 CHILD

WITH APPLE, BERRIES & SEEDS

A delicious combination of whole berries, seeds and chia jam.

For baby's bowl

2 tbsp porridge oats

2 tsp linseeds

4 tbsp milk of your choice

For adult's bowl

25g (¼ cup) porridge oats

4 tbsp linseeds

125ml (½ cup) milk of your choice

For topping (per bowl)

1 tbsp Greek yogurt

1 tsp blackcurrant jam
(see page 234)

1 tbsp spiced apple compote
(see page 41)

5 raspberries

1 tbsp sunflower seeds, crushed

In a microwave-safe bowl, mix the oats, linseeds and milk, then cook in the microwave for 1 minute for baby portion and 1 minute 30 seconds for adult portion.

Allow to cool slightly, then top with a drizzle of Greek yogurt, blackcurrant jam and spiced apple, and sprinkle with raspberries and sunflower seeds.

WITH SUMMER FRUITS

This is a great way to get your children eating more fruit.

For baby's bowl

4 tbsp milk of your choice

¼ dragon fruit

¼ small beetroot

2 tbsp porridge oats

2 tsp linseeds

For adult's bowl

125ml (½ cup) milk of your choice

½ dragon fruit

25g (¼ cup) porridge oats

4 tbsp linseeds

For topping

1 mango, sliced or cut into stars

10 raspberries

4 strawberries

1 kiwi, sliced or cut into stars

10 blueberries

Blend together the milk, dragon fruit and beetroot until brilliantly purple coloured.

Pour into a microwave-safe bowl, then add the oats and linseeds and stir well.

Cook in the microwave for 1 minute.

Allow to cool slightly before topping each bowl with some mango, strawberries, kiwi and blueberries.

MAMMY'S YUMMY PORRIDGE
WITH PEANUT BUTTER, BANANA & NUTTY SPRINKLES

SERVES 1 ADULT & 1 CHILD

This is the one we make the most often and it is Oscar's favourite ever version! (He told me to write that.)

For baby's bowl
2 tbsp porridge oats
2 tsp linseeds
4 tbsp milk of your choice

For adult's bowl
125ml (½ cup) milk of your choice
25g (¼ cup) porridge oats
4 tbsp linseeds

For topping (per bowl)
1 small banana, sliced
1 tsp peanut butter
1 tsp Notella (see page 232)
handful of blueberries
1 tbsp crushed nuts

In a microwave-safe bowl, mix together the oats, linseeds and milk, then cook in the microwave for 1 minute.

Allow to cool slightly before topping with a sliced banana and some peanut butter. Then drizzle over some Notella, add blueberries and sprinkle crushed nuts on top.

AILEEN'S TIP!
You can also make a large pot of porridge by mixing the ingredients in a saucepan and cooking over a medium heat until thickened.

SMASHED AVO
EGGY TOASTIES

MAKES 4

It took three years of persistence and encouragement for Oscar to get a taste for avocado. It's so funny now to watch him devour these avo eggy toasties and ask for more!

3 eggs
60ml (¼ cup) milk of your choice
black pepper
drizzle of rapeseed oil, for frying
4 slices good quality wholegrain bread
1 large avocado, peeled and mashed
4 tsp pesto (see page 220)

Beat the eggs, milk and a sprinkle of black pepper together in a large bowl.

Heat a pan over a medium heat, then drizzle in a little rapeseed oil.

Soak a slice of bread in the egg mixture, then add it to the pan and cook on both sides until golden – roughly 2 minutes per side. Repeat until all of the bread has been used up.

Divide the avocado between the toasties, spread evenly and sprinkle with a little more black pepper.

Drizzle a teaspoon of pesto over each one and serve.

Cut babies' and toddlers' toasties into fingers.

VEGGIE TOASTIES WITH
FRUIT SALAD

SERVES 1 ADULT & 1 CHILD

These toasties are a great way of getting an extra portion of veggies into little ones. Serve with some fruit salad and you have two of their five a day in just one meal!

60ml (¼ cup) milk of your choice
1 red pepper
1 large handful spinach
¼ medium head (1 cup) broccoli, lightly steamed
2 eggs
black pepper, to season
drizzle of rapeseed oil, for frying
4 slices good quality wholegrain bread
1 mango
½ pineapple
1 kiwi
1 clementine
handful of blueberries
1 orange, zest and juice

Add the milk and vegetables to a blender and blend until completely smooth.

Beat the eggs in a large bowl, then pour in the vegetable mixture, sprinkle in a little black pepper and mix well.

Drizzle a little rapeseed oil into a pan over a medium heat, then place a slice of bread into the egg and vegetable mixture. Add to the pan when it is completely soaked through. (You might need to take it out of the bowl with a spatula to prevent the bread breaking apart.)

Fry until golden brown, about 2 minutes per side.

Finely chop all of the fruit and place into a bowl. Squeeze over the orange juice and add the zest, then mix well.

Serve the toasties (cut into fingers for little ones) with some fruit salad on the side.

MACMAMMY
EGG MUFFINS

SERVES 1 ADULT & 1 CHILD

If you keep some English muffins in your freezer, you can reheat them in the toaster (from frozen) and have an amazingly delicious breakfast in less than 10 minutes that the kids will love!

2 tsp rapeseed oil

2 eggs

2 good quality English muffins

2 tsp butter

2 slices Cheddar cheese

Heat the rapeseed oil in a pan.

Lightly oil the inside of a steel cookie cutter, then place onto your pan. Carefully crack an egg into the cutter and gently cook on one side until the egg is set. Remove the cookie cutter, flip the egg over and cook the other side.

Cut the English muffin in half. Toast, then butter it and place on a plate.

Add the cooked egg on top of one half, then a slice of cheese, then place the other half of the muffin on top and serve.

LOADED
BABY OMELETTE

SERVES 2 ADULTS & 2 CHILDREN

Eggs are my go-to breakfast when we are busy and want something really quick. Omelettes can be packed with veggies and goodness and they are filling too. To make them even quicker, prepare the veggies the night before.

2 tbsp rapeseed oil
1 medium white onion, diced
1 bell pepper, diced
1 clove garlic, crushed
6 eggs
black pepper, to season
12 cherry tomatoes, quartered
handful fresh parsley, finely chopped
100g (½ cup) goat's cheese

Add the oil to a frying pan and gently heat.

Fry the onion and pepper until the onions are translucent, then add the garlic and fry for a further minute, until it becomes fragrant.

Take the pan off the heat, then spread the mixture evenly around the pan and leave aside.

Whisk the eggs until smooth and silky, then season with a little pepper.

Pour the egg mixture into the pan, and evenly decorate with the cherry tomatoes and most of the parsley. Finally, scatter chunks of goat's cheese around the omelette.

Place the pan back on a low heat and cook until the bottom starts to turn golden. Use a spatula to lift the side of the omelette up to see how it is progressing.

When the bottom is golden, place the frying pan under the grill (be careful of plastic handles). Cook until the top is set and the cheese has melted. I like mine golden.

Sprinkle the rest of the parsley on top.

Lazy Weekend
BREAKFASTS

Sunday-morning-toddler-hanging-
out-of-your-leg breakfasts that can be
prepared in your own time.

BAKED BELL PEPPERS
WITH EGGS

SERVES 2 ADULTS & 2 CHILDREN

These yummy peppers are super-easy and packed full of nutritious goodness for kids. Get them involved in filling them with veggies and teach them how to crack the egg too. It's fun, although it can get messy!

2 red bell peppers, halved and deseeded

rapeseed oil, for coating

2 large handfuls of spinach leaves, finely chopped

1 large potato, cooked and diced

8 cherry tomatoes, quartered

1 tsp paprika

½ tsp turmeric

black pepper, to season

4 eggs

To serve
sprinkle of Cheddar cheese
handful of chives, finely chopped

Preheat oven to 180°C/350°F/gas 4.

Coat the outside of the peppers with a little rapeseed oil. Place onto a baking tray lined with parchment paper.

Place the spinach, cooked potato, tomatoes, spices and black pepper in a bowl and mix well.

Divide the mixture between the peppers, leaving a dip in the centre of each one.

Crack an egg into each dip, then bake in the oven for 15 minutes, until the eggs are set.

Sprinkle a little Cheddar cheese and chives on top of each to serve.

POTATO &
EGG NESTS

MAKES 12

I normally make this recipe at Easter, but it is so delicious that it can't be just seasonal. The base of the recipe is good enough to have on its own, but we love it with eggs and spinach.

For the nests

4 large potatoes, peeled

1 medium white onion, finely diced

black pepper, to season

4 tbsp rapeseed oil, plus extra for greasing

1 large egg, beaten

For the filling

2 large handfuls of spinach, finely chopped

12 eggs

small handful parsley, finely chopped

Preheat the oven to 180°C/350°F/gas 4.

Grate the potatoes, then place into a clean tea towel and squeeze to remove the moisture.

Add the potatoes to a bowl with the onion, pepper, oil and egg. Stir until fully combined.

Lightly oil a regular-sized muffin tin with a little rapeseed oil, then divide the mixture between the compartments. When you spoon it in, make a hollow in the centre to make the nest, ensuring it comes up the sides.

Add a little chopped spinach to the centre of each nest, then crack an egg into each one.

Bake for 15 minutes, until the eggs are fully set.

To serve, sprinkle a little parsley on top.

AILEEN'S TIP!
Freeze your pancakes! Cook
up a batch, then place a little
parchment paper between
each one and freeze!

CHOCOLATE & BANANA
PANCAKES

MAKES 16

Chocolate and bananas are a match made in heaven – especially for kids. They see these pancakes and just want them, but secretly we have loaded them with so much goodness!

375ml (1½ cups) milk

3 bananas, peeled

2 eggs

2 tsp vanilla extract

4 tbsp melted butter

220g (2 cups) buckwheat flour

4 tsp baking powder

100g (3½oz) good quality raw chocolate, chopped into chunks

rapeseed oil, for frying

To serve

1 tbsp Greek yogurt, per serving

16 raspberries

16 strawberries

16 blackberries

Add the milk, bananas, eggs, vanilla and butter to a blender and blend until smooth and creamy.

Place the buckwheat flour and baking powder into a large bowl and make a well in the centre.

Slowly pour the wet mixture into the well, and whisk into a smooth batter.

Stir in the chocolate chunks.

Heat a pan over a medium heat. Add a very tiny amount of rapeseed oil to the pan (I use kitchen paper to wipe the pan down after I add it).

Use an ice-cream scoop to measure out a serving of batter onto the pan. The pancake should bubble up when one side is done. Then flip it over and cook the other side until golden.

Keep the cooked pancakes warm in the oven until ready to serve. Continue until all the batter is used.

Serve with a dollop of Greek yogurt and topped with berries.

COTTAGE CHEESE
PANCAKES

MAKES 12

High in protein, with a full serving of fruit, these pancakes are a yummy way to start your weekend. These never make it to the freezer because the kids love them too much!

225g (1 cup) cottage cheese
125ml (½ cup) milk
2 eggs
2 tsp vanilla extract
210g (1½ cups) plain or buckwheat flour
2 tsp baking powder
rapeseed oil, for frying

To serve
60ml (¼ cup) Notella
(see page 232)
24 raspberries

Add the cottage cheese, milk, eggs and vanilla to a blender and blend until smooth.

With the blender still running, add the flour one spoonful at a time until it is gone, then add the baking powder.

Heat a little rapeseed oil in a frying pan over a medium heat.

Use an ice-cream scoop to measure out a serving of batter into the pan.

Let the pancake cook until it starts to bubble up, then flip over and cook the other side until golden.

Remove from the pan and transfer to a plate in a warm oven while you repeat until all the batter has been used.

Serve with warm Notella drizzled over and topped with raspberries.

SWEET POTATO
ORANGE PANCAKES

MAKES 16

Don't let the title fool you into thinking these taste like veggies because they don't. In fact, they taste sweet, use no sugar and kids love them. Like, really really love them!

375ml (1½ cups) milk
2 eggs
100g (½ cup) sweet potato purée
½ orange, zest and juice
2 tsp orange oil (optional)
4 tbsp melted butter
220g (2 cups) buckwheat flour
4 tsp baking powder
rapeseed oil, for frying

To serve
60ml (¼ cup) Greek yogurt
2 tbsp good quality raw
chocolate shavings

Add the milk, eggs, potato purée, orange juice (keep the zest for later), orange oil (if using) and melted butter to a blender and whizz until smooth.

Place the flour and baking powder into a bowl, stir well and make a well in the centre.

Gently whisk the wet mixture into the flour until it forms a smooth, silky batter.

Heat a pan with a very small amount of rapeseed oil until hot. Using an ice-cream scoop, add a measure of batter to the pan.

Cook the pancake until the top bubbles up, then flip over and cook the other side until golden.

Remove from the pan and transfer to a plate in a warm oven while you repeat until all the batter has been used.

Serve with a dollop of Greek yogurt, a sprinkle of orange zest and some chocolate shavings for the ultimate healthy treat!

QUINOA
PANCAKES

MAKES 16

These delicious pancakes are perfect for little ones who can't eat either oats or wheat. Or if you just want to try something totally different too!

The night before
220g (1 cup) uncooked quinoa
500ml (2¼ cups) water

For the batter
125ml (½ cup) water
4 tbsp rapeseed oil, plus extra for frying
2 tsp baking powder
1 egg
2 bananas, peeled
2 tsp vanilla extract

To serve
60ml (¼ cup) natural yogurt
16 raspberries
1 banana, peeled and sliced
150g (1½ cups) blueberries

Pour the quinoa into a large bowl and cover with 500ml water. Leave to soak overnight.

The next morning, empty the quinoa into a sieve and rinse under running water for a few moments, until the water runs clear.

Add the quinoa to a blender along with 125ml water. Blend for about 10 minutes, until the quinoa has completely broken up and become a creamy, completely smooth batter.

Add the oil, baking powder, egg, bananas and vanilla to the blender and give everything another whizz until smooth and fully combined.

Heat a drizzle of rapeseed oil in a frying pan over a medium heat, then pour the mixture into small pancakes on the pan.

Cook until you see little bubbles forming then flip and cook the other side until golden.

Serve with natural yogurt and fresh fruit (and if it's the weekend, a little drizzle of good quality maple syrup).

WAFFLES & CHOCOLATE
NICE CREAM

MAKES 8

Crispy and delicious, these are a huge hit with my kids and are easy to make too. Perfect for when you have a little time in the kitchen.

For the waffles
220g (2 cups) buckwheat flour
3 tsp baking powder
2 eggs
430ml (1¾ cups) milk of your choice
6 tbsp melted butter

For the nice cream
2 sliced bananas, frozen
1 tablespoon cacao powder
2 tbsp milk of your choice
1 tsp sprinkles to serve

Whisk together the flour and baking powder.

In a jug, beat the eggs, milk and butter, then pour over the flour mixture and whisk into a smooth batter.

Heat your waffle maker. You may have to use a pastry brush to lightly coat it with rapeseed oil to prevent sticking – the butter in the batter should be enough but try it to see.

Pour in about 180ml (⅓ cup) of batter per waffle and cook according to the manufacturer's instructions.

To make the banana nice cream, add the banana, cacao powder and milk to a high-speed blender and whizz until it resembles a smooth soft-serve ice cream.

Spoon the nice cream on top of the waffles and serve straight away.

Xs AND Os WAFFLES WITH
RASPBERRIES & BLUEBERRIES

MAKES 8

This is a fun way to get kids eating fruit – play Xs and Os with waffles! My toddler is so smart he always wins...

220g (2 cups) buckwheat flour
3 tsp baking powder
2 eggs
430ml (1¾ cups) milk of your choice
6 tbsp melted butter

To serve
12 blueberries
12 raspberries
Greek yogurt
blackberry jam (see page 234)

Whisk the flour and baking powder together.

In a jug, beat the eggs, milk and butter, then pour over the flour mixture and whisk into a smooth batter.

Heat your waffle maker. You may have to use a pastry brush to lightly coat it with rapeseed oil to prevent sticking – the butter in the batter should be enough but try it to see.

Pour in about 180ml (⅓ cup) of batter per waffle and cook according to the manufacturer's instructions.

To serve, take 6 pieces of fruit each and take turns to place in the waffle squares, trying to get three in a row! Top with Greek yogurt then drizzle over a little blackberry jam.

Animal
TOASTIES

This is not a recipe as such, but it's a cute way of serving toast with fruit to your little ones. It is also perfect for letting your kids help – although they might tell you they have made a giraffe that looks nothing like one. Just go with it!

CAT TOASTY

1 slice wholegrain brown bread, toasted then cut into a circle. Spread over a little peanut butter or sunflower seed butter. Slice a strawberry for the ears and nose, then add 2 blueberries for eyes.

FOX TOASTY

1 slice wholegrain brown bread, toasted then cut into a circle. Spread 3/4s of the toast with cream cheese and the center with peanut butter. Use 2 slices of banana with a blueberry on each for the eyes, 1 blueberry for a nose and a half slice of banana for the ears.

1 slice wholegrain brown bread, toasted then cut into a circle. Spread the bread with cream cheese. Slice 2 strawberries thinly then place as shown for the gills. Use 1 slice of banana for the eye with a blueberry on top. Then cut 1 slice of banana in half for the tail.

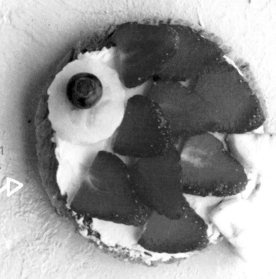

MONKEY TOASTY

1 slice wholegrain brown bread, toasted then cut into a circle. Spread over some Notella (see page 232). Use 2 blueberries for eyes. Then slice a banana into thin slices and use as shown for the mouth and ears.

OWL TOASTY

1 slice wholegrain brown bread, toasted then cut into a circle. Spread the bread with peanut butter. Use 2 slices of banana for eyes with blueberries on top, then 2 slices of strawberry for the wings. Cut a small piece from another strawberry slice for the beak.

Lunchbox
WONDERS

I will put my hands up and admit that lunches totally stress me out. It can be hard to come up with something that isn't a repetitive cheese or egg salad sambo. So the challenge was on for me to create a mix of lunches that kids of all ages – and mums and dads too – would be excited about eating.

There is something really lovely about getting children involved in the planning of lunches too. It really puts the onus on them to eat the food they bring to crèche or school and be proud of their efforts.

ALL YOU NEED IS 10 RECIPES

While this section of the book contains over 20 recipes, I want you to pick your top 10 – it really helps if you do it with your child. Write them up in the lunchbox wonders cut-out planner (page 112), then stick it on your fridge. The aim is to have a two-week rotation of recipes, so your child (and you!) should only be eating the same lunch twice a month and you will never have to think about lunchboxes again. Ever! Sound appealing? It does to me!

Throughout the book, I have also highlighted some other recipes that are great for lunchboxes, so you can choose from those if you can't pick 10 recipes from this section. I have included a handy list of fruit choices too. Get your little ones to pick five of their favourite fruits and make them a daily thing: Mango Mondays, Tangerine Tuesdays, Watermelon Wednesdays – I can't think of Thursdays, but you get my drift!

PIZZA
TOASTIES

MAKES 4

I only make proper pizza dough at weekends when I have some time on my hands. This recipe might be sacrilege to some, but kids love it and it is a super way of getting them to eat lots of veggies. It is also really quick to make and perfect for lunchboxes too.

4 slices good quality wholegrain bread
3 tbsp tomato purée
1 clove garlic, crushed
1 tbsp water
black pepper, to season
1 red bell pepper, sliced
10 black olives, sliced
2 large tomatoes, sliced
150g (½ cup) buffalo mozzarella (or a good white Cheddar cheese)

Preheat oven to 180°C/350°F/gas 4.

Put the bread onto a baking tray, then place in the oven for 5 minutes.

While the bread is toasting, add the tomato purée, garlic and water to a bowl and stir really well. Season with a little black pepper.

Remove the toast from the oven. It should be slightly browned on one side. Flip the slices over, then divide the sauce between them, making sure to spread right to the sides and corners.

Divide the pepper, olives and tomatoes between the toasties. Break apart the cheese and scatter on top.

Bake in the oven for 8–10 minutes, until the cheese is fully melted.

Serve warm or cold.

SWEET POTATO & CARROT
CURRIED HUMMUS WITH
10-MINUTE FALAFELS

SERVES 2 ADULTS & 2 CHILDREN

My friend Kerry told me her lovely little daughter Éabha loves anything orange, so I made this hummus especially for her. She loved it so much that I had to include it here for you to try. It is very lightly spiced and super creamy, plus it is packed with veggies, so it's amazing for little kids.

For the hummus

1 large sweet potato, roasted with skin on for 40 minutes until soft

4 carrots, roasted

4 cloves garlic, roasted

400g (15oz) tinned chickpeas

4 tbsp tahini

4 tbsp olive oil

4 tbsp water

1 lemon, juice only

1 tsp ground coriander

1 tsp ground cumin

½ tsp ground turmeric

¼ tsp ground cinnamon

3 stalks fresh coriander

For the falafel

400g tinned chickpeas

1 clove garlic, crushed

2 shallots, finely diced

1 tsp ground cumin

2 tbsp flour of your choice

2–3 stalks fresh coriander, finely chopped

3 tbsp rapeseed oil

Preheat oven to 180°C/350°F/gas 4.

Place all of the ingredients for the hummus into a high-speed blender and blend until really smooth and silky. Add more water (1 tbsp at a time) if it is too thick.

Pour the hummus into little bowls and leave in the fridge while you make the falafel.

Add the ingredients for the falafel, except the oil, to a clean blender and blend until it resembles breadcrumbs, then slowly pour in the oil and blend again. It should come together like a dough.

Shape into small falafel shapes, then place on a baking tray lined with greaseproof paper.

Bake for 12 minutes or until the falafels are golden and cooked through.

Serve with the hummus.

VEGGIE-LOADED
MINI QUICHES

MAKES 12

I am a huge fan of quiches, as are my kids. They are great lunchbox fillers, easy to make and freeze well, so what is not to love? This recipe is delicious and chock-full of veggie goodness so it's great for little ones of all ages.

For the pastry
150g (1 cup) plain flour
80g (⅓ cup) butter
2–3 tbsp water

For the filling
2 tbsp rapeseed oil
24 sweet cherry tomatoes
8 cloves garlic, skins on
1 courgette, finely sliced into circles
1 medium-sized onion, finely sliced
6 eggs
sprinkle of pepper
1 tsp sweet paprika

sprinkle of Cheddar for each one

Preheat oven to 180°C/350°F/gas 4.

To make the pastry, sift the flour into a bowl then, using your fingers, work the butter in until the flour starts to resemble fine breadcrumbs. Add the water a tbsp at a time until the pastry comes together. Wrap in cling film and refrigerate for about 30 minutes.

Place the pastry onto a lightly floured surface and roll until it measures about 0.5cm deep. Then cut out 12 circles to fit a standard muffin tin.

Lightly butter a muffin tin and line each cup with a pastry case, then place in the fridge.

To make the filling, drizzle the rapeseed oil over a baking tray, then add the cherry tomatoes, garlic, courgette and onion. Bake for 25 minutes, until the vegetables are almost cooked but not totally soft.

Remove from the oven and take out the garlic cloves. Remove their skins, then use a spoon to mash the flesh into a spreadable paste.

In a bowl, whisk the eggs, pepper, paprika and garlic paste until light and bubbly.

Remove the pastry-lined tin from the fridge. Divide the vegetable mix between the pastry cases, then fill with the egg mixture and top with a sprinkle of cheese.

Bake for 25 minutes or until the pastry is golden and the egg has fully set.

Remove from the tin and cool on a wire rack before serving.

CHICKEN & CHEESE
QUESADILLAS

MAKES 4

What's not to love about quesadillas? They're wraps with so much tasty goodness that your little one's lunchbox is definitely going to come home empty! You can make the filling ahead of time and freeze, so putting these together will take all of 5 mins!

For the make-ahead sauce

drizzle of rapeseed oil

1 red onion, finely sliced

1 red bell pepper, finely sliced

4 tbsp tomato purée

1 tsp ground cumin

1 tsp ground coriander

1 tsp sweet paprika

2 tbsp water

For the quesadillas

2 cooked chicken breasts (or 400g [15oz] tinned black beans)

4 good quality tortilla mini-wraps

sprinkle of Cheddar cheese per wrap

small bunch fresh coriander, finely chopped

1 avocado, sliced, with a dash of lime juice to prevent browning, to serve

Heat the rapeseed oil in a frying pan, then add the onion and pepper and fry until the onion has become translucent, about 2–3 minutes.

Add the tomato purée, spices and water and stir well. The sauce should be thick.

Use 2 forks to shred the chicken, then add to the sauce and stir well. You can cool and freeze the sauce at this point to save for busy days.

When you're ready to assemble the quesadillas, heat a dry frying pan over a medium heat.

Place a tortilla onto the pan, sprinkle half with cheese, then top with a few heaped tablespoons of the sauce and chicken mix, and sprinkle over the fresh coriander.

Cook for about 2 minutes, then fold the empty side of the tortilla over to make a half-circle shape.

Flip the tortilla over to heat up the other side, then remove from the pan and cut into triangles.

Serve with slices of avocado.

 MAKE IT VEGETARIAN: Swap chicken for a portion of kidney beans.

ITALIAN
QUINOA BITES

MAKES 24

I published a variation of these on my site and they were a huge success.
They are perfect for little babies and are great for vegetarian kids too because
they are really high in protein!

200g (1 cup) quinoa, rinsed

500ml (2 cups) homemade chicken/vegetable stock or water

4 tbsp rapeseed oil

1 medium onion, finely diced

1 red pepper, finely diced

1 medium courgette, finely diced

2 cloves garlic, crushed

10 basil leaves, finely chopped

1 tsp dried oregano

2 eggs

2 tbsp tomato purée

Preheat oven to 180°C/350°F/gas 4.

Add the quinoa to a pot with the stock or water and cook as per the instructions on the packet. Once cooked leave aside to cool.

Heat 2 tbsp of the rapeseed oil in a frying pan over a medium heat and gently fry the onion until translucent.

Add the pepper and courgette and fry until soft and cooked through. Add the garlic and cook for a further 3 minutes, then stir in the basil and oregano. Set aside to cool.

In a bowl, whisk together the eggs, tomato purée and 2 more tbsp rapeseed oil until fully combined. Then add the cooked quinoa and vegetables and mix well.

Form into 24 evenly sized balls and place on a baking sheet lined with parchment paper.

Bake for 25 minutes.

Eat warm or cold!

CHICKEN ON A STICK WITH
PEANUT SAUCE

MAKES 8

If it's on a stick, my kids love it! Seriously, and I'm not the only one – I get a lot of mails from people telling me this trick works wonders for getting kids to eat more veggies. These are yummy when cold too, so they work great in a lunchbox and can be made the night before. I switch up the chicken for tofu for Dylan, my vegetarian 11-year-old.

For the skewers
4 chicken breasts, cut into chunks
1 red bell pepper, cut into chunks
1 courgette, sliced thickly
½ pineapple, cut into chunks

For the sauce
½ pineapple
2 tbsp soy sauce
125ml (½ cup) smooth peanut butter
½ lime, juice only
1 clove garlic
black pepper, to season

Preheat oven to 180°C/350°F/gas 4.

Soak 8 wooden skewers in water while you prepare the ingredients.

Place the chicken into a bowl with the vegetables and pineapple.

Place all of the ingredients for the sauce into a blender and blend until really smooth and creamy.

Pour over the chicken and vegetables, then use your hands to coat them fully. You can leave this to marinate overnight if you like.

Take the skewers out of the water, then add a piece of chicken, pepper, courgette and pineapple to each one. Repeat until the skewers are full, with just a little piece left at the top and bottom for children to hold.

Place onto a baking tray lined with parchment paper, then bake in the oven for 30 minutes, until the chicken is cooked through.

Serve warm or cold.

AILEEN'S TIP!
Swap the smooth peanut butter for tahini to make a nut-free sauce.

SWEET POTATO &
CAULIFLOWER CAKES

MAKES 12

Soft, delicious, easy to make and perfect for the freezer too, these yummy cakes are brilliant for babies, toddlers and kids of all ages.

2 large sweet potatoes, cooked (I roast mine with skins on for 40 minutes then discard the skins)

1 head cauliflower, cooked (I roast mine for 30 minutes until soft)

handful fresh coriander, finely chopped

2 eggs

100g (¾ cup) plain flour

1 tsp ground cumin

1 tsp ground coriander

rapeseed oil, for frying

In a large bowl, mash the sweet potatoes and cauliflower with a fork. Don't use a blender or it will become soggy.

Add the fresh coriander, eggs, flour, cumin and ground coriander, then use your hands to mix really well. If the mixture is too wet, just add a little more flour until it comes together.

Form into potato-cake shapes about 6cm in diameter and 1.5cm high.

Heat a light drizzle of oil in a pan over a medium heat. Add the cakes to the pan in batches and fry until golden. Flip them over and repeat until they are cooked through.

BABY-FRIENDLY
VEGGIE FRITTERS

MAKES 12

I made a version of these in my first book, *The Baby-Led Feeding Cookbook*, and they were a huge hit with children – especially little ones starting on their food journey. This is another yummy version with a new mix of veggies and spices that I hope you will love as much as the original!

100g (2 cups) carrot, peeled and grated

100g (2 cups) sweet potato, peeled and grated

100g (1 cup) cauliflower, very finely chopped

1 clove garlic, crushed

1 tsp ground cumin

1 tsp ground coriander

1 bunch fresh coriander, finely chopped

4 tbsp flour

2 eggs

pinch black pepper

rapeseed oil, for brushing

Preheat oven to 190°C/375°F/gas 5.

Add all of the ingredients, except the oil, to a large bowl and mix until fully combined.

Shape into patties and place on a baking sheet lined with parchment paper.

Lightly brush the tops of each patty with a little oil then bake for 12 minutes.

Take out of the oven and flip over. Lightly brush the tops of the unbaked sides with oil then bake for another 12 minutes or until golden.

BEANS, BEANS,
GOOD FOR THE HEART SALAD

SERVES 2 ADULTS & 2 CHILDREN

I taught my kids the 'beans, beans, good for the heart' rhyme – and, yes, their favourite part is the farting bit (I know, I'm very childish). They don't mention that when they go to school, but they love bringing this salad, and it makes me smile every single time.

400g (15oz) tinned black beans

400g (15oz) tinned red kidney beans

400g (15oz) tinned butter beans

1 large red bell pepper, finely diced

1 large yellow bell pepper, finely diced

1 large sweet onion, finely diced

140g (1 cup) peas
(I use cooked frozen peas)

bunch fresh coriander, finely chopped

60ml (¼ cup) balsamic vinegar

60ml (¼ cup) extra virgin olive oil

3 tbsp maple syrup

1 clove garlic, crushed

black pepper, to season

Drain the beans and put into a large bowl.

Add the peppers, onion, peas and coriander.

Place a pot over a low heat and add the vinegar, oil, maple syrup and garlic. Heat until it starts to bubble, then simmer gently for about 3 minutes, until the garlic cooks. Season with black pepper, to taste.

Pour the sauce over the beans, cover and refrigerate until ready to serve.

KID-APPROVED
PASTA SALAD

SERVES 2 ADULTS & 2 CHILDREN

This is a super-easy salad to make and stores well in the freezer too – just leave out the mozzarella until you are ready to eat. I use a mix of vegetables that my kids like, so this lunch is always eaten.

300g (3 cups) pasta shells
140g (1 cup) frozen peas
20 cherry tomatoes
1 sweet red onion
1 sweet red pepper, chopped
200g (½ cup) mozzarella balls
4 heaped tbsp pesto
(see page 220)

Heat a large pot of water until boiling, then add the pasta and cook for about 8 minutes, until almost soft.

Add the peas to the pasta pot and cook for another couple of minutes, until the peas are tender, then empty the pot into a colander in the sink to drain fully. Run the pasta and peas under the cold tap for a few minutes, until the pasta is really cold.

Chop the tomatoes into quarters, finely chop the red onion and pepper, then add to a large bowl along with the mozzarella balls and pesto.

Toss the salad really well to make sure the pasta is fully coated.

Store in the fridge until ready to use. Serve cold.

FRUIT & VEGGIE SALAD WITH
GREEK YOGURT AND GRANOLA

SERVES 2 ADULTS & 2 CHILDREN

Most children love fruit so this recipe is a great way to pack lots of goodness into a lunchbox with zero arguments. I always like to sneak a few sweet veggies in there too, and because it's so colourful the kids barely notice! Our lunchboxes are divided into sections, so I put the yogurt, granola and fruit in separate compartments and then the kids can put them together in school.

2 kiwis, peeled and chopped

4 clementines, peeled and segmented

1 pomegranate, deseeded

1 ripe mango, peeled and chopped

2 raw carrots, grated

1 raw beetroot, grated

10 fresh mint leaves, finely chopped

1 lime, juice only

To serve (per portion)

125ml (½ cup) Greek yogurt

2 tbsp Nut & Sugar-Free Fruit Granola (see page 34)

Place all of the prepared fruit and veg in a bowl. Add the mint leaves and lime juice.

Stir well and leave covered in a refrigerator until ready to use.

When serving, top with Greek yogurt and granola.

SWEET POTATO & CARROT
SUPERHERO MUFFINS

MAKES 32

These gorgeous muffins contain plenty of veggies, and even though you may think they are savoury they are actually sweet. The kids love them in their lunchboxes.

300g (2 cups) plain flour
2 tsp baking powder
1 tsp ground cinnamon
½ tsp ground nutmeg
½ tsp ground ginger
100g (½ cup) puréed sweet potato
100g (½ cup) puréed carrot
250ml milk (1 cup)
2 eggs
60ml (¼ cup) rapeseed oil
1 tsp vanilla extract

Preheat oven to 170°C/340°F/gas 3.

Add flour, baking powder and spices to a bowl and stir. Make a well in the centre then set aside.

In a separate bowl beat together the sweet potato, carrot, milk, eggs, rapeseed oil and vanilla.

Slowly pour the wet mixture into the flour and whisk until fully combined and silky smooth.

Divide the batter between lightly oiled mini-muffin moulds.

Bake for 15–20 minutes until browned and a wooden skewer comes out clean.

Serve warm or cold.

VEGGIE-LOADED
MINI MUFFINS

MAKES 32

As a mum, I feel really good about my kids skipping into school with a few of these in their lunchboxes. They are packed with veggies, yet my little ones never seem to notice. Probably because they taste so good!

3 carrots, grated

1 courgette, grated

2 medium shallots, finely diced

80g (½ cup) cauliflower, finely chopped

2 eggs, beaten

60ml (¼ cup) rapeseed oil

250ml (1 cup) milk

60g (¼ cup) Cheddar cheese, grated

300g (2 cups) flour

2 tsp baking powder

Preheat oven to 160°C/325°F/gas 3.

Add all of the vegetables to a large bowl, then stir in the eggs, oil, milk and cheese until the mixture is smooth.

Slowly beat in the flour and baking powder until it forms a batter.

Scoop evenly into a lightly oiled mini-muffin tin and bake for 25 minutes, until a skewer comes out clean.

TODDLER-AND-KID-APPROVED
BANANA AND WALNUT MUFFINS

MAKES 24 MINI AND 4 LARGE

This recipe is a huge hit on the Baby-Led Feeding website so it really had to go into the book. While these muffins taste sweet, they are actually completely sugar free and perfect for babies, toddlers and teenagers too. Make a large batch and freeze!

300g (2 cups) plain flour

2 tsp baking powder

60g (½ cup) walnuts, ground

3 bananas, chopped

250ml (1 cup) milk

2 eggs

60ml (¼ cup) rapeseed oil

1 tsp vanilla extract

2 lemons, zest of 1 and juice of both

Preheat oven to 170°C/340°F/gas 3.

Add flour, baking powder and ground walnuts to a bowl and stir. Make a well in the centre and set aside.

In a separate bowl, mash the bananas until smooth. Add the remaining ingredients and stir really well until it becomes creamy.

Slowly pour the wet mixture into the flour and whisk until fully combined and silky smooth.

Spoon the batter into a lightly oiled mini-muffin tin. I usually have enough batter left over to make 4 large muffins too.

Bake for 15–20 minutes, until browned and a wooden skewer comes out clean.

Serve warm or cold.

VEGGIE
PIZZA SCROLLS

MAKES 10

One of my youngest's number one lunches. These pastry scrolls are filled with delicious vegetables and cheese and are nourishing and filling too. Expect empty lunchboxes coming home!

For the pastry
150g (1 cup) plain flour
50g (¼ cup) butter
4 tbsp water

For the sauce
3 tbsp tomato purée
1 clove garlic, crushed
2 tbsp water
black pepper, to season

1 red bell pepper, finely diced
2 large handfuls spinach, roughly chopped
2 handfuls frozen peas
2 handfuls frozen corn
50g (¼ cup) goat's cheese

Preheat oven to 180°C/350°F/gas 4.

In a bowl, sift the flour, then add the butter and, using your fingers, rub into the flour until it resembles fine breadcrumbs. Adtd the water 1 tbsp at a time, mixing into the flour and butter until the pastry comes together.

Roll into a rectangular shape, about 0.5cm thick, on a floured surface.

Add the tomato purée, crushed garlic and water to a bowl and season lightly with pepper. Stir until smooth.

Evenly spread the sauce over the pastry, then sprinkle over the red pepper, spinach, peas and corn.

Pick up the shorter side of the pastry and roll up as tightly and gently as possible.

Cut the roll into 10 even slices, then place into a regular-sized, lightly oiled muffin tin.

Sprinkle over the goat's cheese and bake for 25 minutes.

Allow to cool a little before serving. Can be eaten warm or cold.

OAT PANCAKES WITH
BLUEBERRIES

MAKES 12

Make these pancakes weeks before and store in the freezer with a little parchment paper between them. When you want to use one, just take it out of the freezer and pop into your little one's lunchbox – it will have defrosted by lunchtime!

250ml (1 cup) milk of your choice
1 egg
135g (1½ cups) oats
1 tsp baking powder
2 tbsp melted butter
2 bananas
1 tsp vanilla extract
250g (2½ cups) blueberries
rapeseed oil, for frying

Place all of the ingredients (except the blueberries and oil) into a blender in the order they are listed. It is important that the milk goes in first, as it helps to break up the oats and other ingredients. Blend until smooth.

Stir in the blueberries with a spatula.

Heat a pan over a medium heat, then add a very small amount of rapeseed oil to coat the pan.

Use an ice-cream scoop to portion out the pancakes onto the pan. Cook each one until it starts to bubble up, then flip over and cook the other side.

Serve warm or cold.

OVERNIGHT
CARROT-CAKE OATS

SERVES 1 ADULT & 1 CHILD

I have overnight oats in the breakfast section of the book, but I wanted to put these here to remind you that they are super for lunchboxes too. This recipe especially is a great way to get two portions of veggies and fruit into your kids, which is exactly what they need when they are in school.

90g (1 cup) oats

2 medium carrots, finely grated

40g (¼ cup) raisins

250ml (1 cup) milk of your choice

2 bananas

1 tsp cinnamon

1 tbsp Greek yogurt

2 tbsp pecan nuts, toasted on a dry frying pan then crushed

Place the oats, carrots and raisins into bowl.

Add the milk, bananas and cinnamon to a blender and blend until smooth and creamy, then pour over the oats and stir well.

Place into jars, then top with the yogurt and crushed pecan nuts, cover and leave in the fridge overnight.

SUPER-HANDY
PIES

MAKES 12

Perfect for little hands and packed full of goodness – you'll end up making these pies again and again! They are great for the freezer – just take out the night before to defrost.

For the pastry
200g (2 cups) plain flour
160g (⅔ cup) butter
3-4 tbsp water

For the filling
2 tbsp rapeseed oil
1 red onion, finely diced
2 cloves garlic, crushed
1 medium butternut squash, peeled and cut into 1 inch pieces
1 courgette, cut into 1 inch pieces
200g (7oz) tinned tomatoes
3 tbsp tomato purée
1 tsp ground cumin
1 tsp ground coriander
400g (15oz) tinned haricot beans (or white or regular kidney beans)

Preheat oven to 180°C/350°F/gas 4.

To make the pastry, sift the flour into a bowl then, using your fingers, work the butter in until the flour starts to resemble fine breadcrumbs. Add the water a tablespoon at a time until the pastry comes together. Wrap in cling film and refrigerate for about 30 minutes.

To make the filling, drizzle a baking dish with the rapeseed oil, then add the rest of the ingredients.

Bake in the oven for 30 minutes, or until the butternut squash is super soft, then remove and allow to cool.

Roll the pastry out until it is about 0.5cm thick, then cut into small bowl-sized circles, roughly 10cm in diameter. Add a heaped tbsp of the filling to each one, brush the sides with a little beaten egg, then fold over and seal. Prick the top of each pastry with a fork, then bake for 25 minutes until golden brown.

Serve warm or cold.

BROWN BREAD
ROLL-UPS

MAKES 4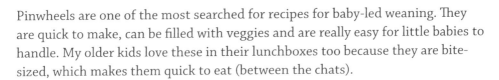

Pinwheels are one of the most searched for recipes for baby-led weaning. They are quick to make, can be filled with veggies and are really easy for little babies to handle. My older kids love these in their lunchboxes too because they are bite-sized, which makes them quick to eat (between the chats).

4 slices wholemeal bread

4 tsp hummus

½ tsp linseeds per slice

large handful baby salad leaves, finely chopped

3 cherry tomatoes, finely chopped

4 slices cucumber, finely chopped

Cut the crusts off each slice of bread and use a rolling pin to roll completely flat.

Add a tsp of hummus to each slice then sprinkle over the linseeds and add a little salad, some cherry tomatoes and cucumber.

Roll up each piece of bread, then cut into bite-sized slices and serve.

PBJ SAMBO
ROLL-UPS

SERVES 1

This one is for my American friends and fans: the good old peanut butter and jelly sambo – my healthy take, though, obviously. A real winner with kids, and once you try it yourself, you'll understand why.

1 slice wholegrain bread

1 tbsp peanut butter

1 tbsp blackcurrant jam (see page 234)

Cut the crusts from the slice of bread then use a rolling pin to roll completely flat.

Spread the peanut butter on first, then top with jam.

Roll into a long roll, then slice into bite-sized pieces.

Lunchbox PLANNER

	MONDAY	TUESDAY	WEDNESDAY
Week 1			
Week 2			
Week 3			
Week 4			

Use this handy planner to organise your entire month of lunch boxes. Simply go through this book and pick your top 10 lunches, then rotate them on a fortnightly basis. It saves so much time and takes away all of the stress associated with school lunches.

THURSDAY	FRIDAY	My Top 10 LUNCHES
		Oatmeal Power Cookies page 27
		Veggie Toasties with Fruit Salad page 52
		Pizza Toasties page 77
		Italian Quinoa Bites page 82
		Kid-Approved Pasta Salad page 92
		Quinoa Falafels in a Bowl of Yum page 150
		Whatever's In the Fridge Hummus with Veggies and Pittas page 174
		Healthy Strawberry Blondies page 239
		Nut-Free Baby Flapjacks page 262
		Sugar-Free Chocolate Chunky Mini Muffins page 277

What's for
DINNER?

This is the eternal question in most homes, including mine! It can be hard to keep things different and original, but with a good healthy quantity of veggies too.

Dinner can be a real struggle for parents – it's hard to cook with a toddler hanging out of your leg, and maybe even a baby in a sling at the same time. We need an arsenal of dinners that aren't too complicated to make and that everyone will enjoy!

To help, I've broken this section into 3 parts:

I Need Dinner Now!

Cook Once, Eat Twice Dinners

Weekend Dinners

I Need Dinner
NOW!

Delicious baby-friendly family dinners that can be rustled up in less than 20 minutes.

This does not mean that you have to be able to speed-chop onions to get it done in this time, but it does mean that you may have to prepare a few things beforehand. Believe me, it's worth it to have some sauces in the fridge or freezer ready to go.

PESTO PASTA WITH
GRILLED VEGGIES & BALSAMIC TOMATOES

SERVES 2 ADULTS & 2 CHILDREN

Kids love pasta and it's a perfect dish to load plenty of veggies into while still keeping it child friendly. We cook this dish every week – sometimes even twice a week!

350g (12oz) wholewheat pasta
2 red bell peppers, deseeded and cut into 8 spears each
drizzle of olive oil
2 courgettes

For the pesto
70g (3 cups) basil leaves
100g (¾ cup) pine nuts
125ml (½ cup) olive oil
cracked black pepper, to taste
2 cloves garlic

For the balsamic tomatoes
16 cherry tomatoes, quartered
2 tbsp balsamic vinegar
2 tbsp olive oil

Cook the pasta as per the instructions on the pack.

While the pasta is cooking, drizzle the peppers with a little olive oil and place skin side up on a baking tray. Grill under a high heat until the skin starts to char. This takes about 5 minutes. Flip the peppers over and cook the other side, then remove, place in a bowl and cover with cling film. This helps to remove the skins, making them easy for little ones to manage.

When the peppers are covered, slice the courgette lengthways, drizzle with a little olive oil and place under the grill on a medium heat. Grill until one side starts to brown. This only takes about 5 minutes so keep an eye on them to make sure they don't burn. I don't flip over as they're usually cooked enough for little hands at this stage.

Next, peel the grilled peppers, then chop them and the courgettes into small pieces.

Meanwhile, put all the ingredients for the pesto into a blender and blend until it becomes a smooth and silky sauce. Pour the sauce into a pan and place over a medium heat. Stir for a few minutes until it becomes deliciously fragrant, then add the cooked vegetables.

The pasta should be cooked at this stage so drain it and add to the pan with the pesto and grilled vegetables. Toss until every piece of pasta is covered.

Put the cherry tomatoes into a bowl with the vinegar and oil. Stir well, then spoon over the pasta, drizzling over any remaining dressing.

Place everything on the table and dig in!

PATATAS BRAVAS WITH
CHICKEN/BEANS

SERVES 2 ADULTS & 2 CHILDREN

One of the tastiest and quickest dinners you will ever eat. Plates will be licked clean, guaranteed!

3 chicken fillets or 800g (28oz) tinned black beans

drizzle olive oil

1 tsp sweet paprika

For the potatoes

2 tbsp rapeseed oil

1kg (35oz) baby potatoes, boiled

1 tbsp garlic powder

1 tbsp onion powder

For the tomato sauce

1 onion, finely diced

drizzle of olive oil

1 clove garlic, crushed

400g (14oz) tinned chopped tomatoes

black pepper, to season

For the lemon and garlic sauce

125ml (½ cup) Greek yogurt

juice 1 lemon

1 small clove garlic (roasted until soft for babies), crushed

small handful fresh chives, chopped, to serve

Preheat oven to 180°C/350°F/gas 4.

Place the chicken fillets on a baking tray lined with parchment paper. Sprinkle the paprika over them, drizzle with the olive oil and use your fingers to spread it evenly over the meat. Bake for about 30 minutes, until cooked through. Slice and leave aside.

If you're using beans instead, heat the oil in a saucepan, add the paprika and beans and heat until warmed through.

Heat the rapeseed oil in a frying pan over a high heat. Add the potatoes and fry until golden brown. You can also put them in the oven at 180°C/350°F/gas 4 for 30 minutes until they go super-crispy.

Add the garlic and onion powder and stir well.

To make the tomato sauce, add the onion and olive oil to a pan and cook until the onion is translucent. Add the garlic and cook for a further 2 minutes before adding the tomatoes. Heat the sauce through, then season to your liking with a little pepper.

To make the lemon and garlic sauce, simply add all the ingredients to a small bowl and give it a good stir.

Serve the potatoes with a little tomato sauce over them, some chicken or beans on top, then drizzle with the lemon and garlic sauce and a sprinkling of chives.

 MAKE IT VEGETARIAN: Swap chicken for a portion of black beans or chickpeas.

AILEEN'S TIP!
Shred chicken for a baby-friendly dinner.

SALMON AND PRAWN
LINGUINE

SERVES 2 ADULTS & 2 CHILDREN

Seafood linguine has always been a real comfort food for me, and it is my go-to dish when I am rushing in from work with hungry children looking for food now!

200g (7oz) linguine (or spaghetti)

2 salmon fillets

For the sauce

2 tbsp rapeseed oil

1 large onion, finely chopped

2 cloves garlic, crushed

80ml (⅓ cup) natural yogurt

80ml (⅓ cup) whole milk

50g (¼ cup) blue cheese (I use Tipperary Blue) or goat's cheese

For the prawns

knob of butter

1 clove garlic

200g (7oz) cooked king prawns

small bunch fresh parsley, finely chopped

10 cherry tomatoes, roasted

Bring a large pot of water to the boil, add the pasta and cook for 10 minutes, until soft and cooked through.

At the same time, steam the salmon by cutting it up into small cubes and placing in a steamer over the pasta. It should be cooked through and light pink when done.

Meanwhile, heat the rapeseed oil in a frying pan. Fry the onion until it becomes soft and translucent, then add the garlic, cooking until it is lovely and fragrant but not browning.

Place the onion and garlic in a blender with the yogurt and milk, blend until smooth and creamy, then pour back into the pan.

Roughly crumble in the cheese and stir well over a low heat until fully melted, then remove the pan from the heat.

In a separate pan, melt the knob of butter (roughly a heaped teaspoon) over a medium to low heat. Then add the garlic and prawns and cook for about 2 minutes, until the prawns are warmed through.

To serve, drain the linguine and add to the pan with the sauce. Toss until completely coated, then flake in the salmon and add the prawns. Give everything a good stir and sprinkle with the fresh parsley. Place the roasted cherry tomatoes on top and serve.

THAI FISHCAKES WITH
POTATO SQUARES

SERVES 2 ADULTS & 2 CHILDREN

If you have ever wondered how to get your child to eat more fish, then this is the recipe for you. These little fish cakes are tasty, easy to make and delicious.

For the potato squares

4 large Russet potatoes, washed and cut into cubes

drizzle of rapeseed oil

1 sprig rosemary, leaves finely chopped

For the fish cakes

drizzle of rapeseed oil

1 medium red onion, roughly chopped

2 cloves garlic, crushed

1 lime, juice and zest

1 tsp ground turmeric

1 tsp ground cumin

1 tsp ground coriander

2 large hake fillets (or fish of your choice), deboned

1 egg

large handful fresh coriander

2 tbsp flour of your choice (I use buckwheat)

15 green beans, finely sliced

50g (1 cup) breadcrumbs of your choice

To serve

2 tbsp Greek yogurt

juice ¼ lime

small bunch fresh parsley, finely chopped

Preheat oven to 180°C/350°F/gas 4.

Place the potatoes on a baking tray lined with parchment paper. Drizzle with some rapeseed oil, sprinkle over the rosemary leaves and use your hands to completely coat the potatoes.

Bake for 30 minutes, until golden.

While the potatoes are cooking, heat some more rapeseed oil in a frying pan, add the onion and fry until golden. Add the garlic and fry for a further 2 minutes, until cooked.

Spoon the onion mixture into a food processor along with the lime juice and zest, spices, fish, egg and fresh coriander.

Blend until smooth, then transfer into a large bowl along with the flour and the green beans, and stir well.

Form into small fishcakes, then roll in the breadcrumbs. Repeat until all the mixture is used up.

Fry in a little rapeseed oil until golden on both sides and cooked through.

Serve with a little Greek yogurt mixed with lime juice, and sprinkle with parsley to garnish.

BAKED PESTO HADDOCK WITH
GARLIC SPUDS

SERVES 2 ADULTS & 2 CHILDREN

We try to eat fish once a week, and this dish is one of our favourites. Easy and quick, and great for the freezer too!

4 fillets haddock

4 tbsp Basil and Spinach Pesto (see page 220)

4 tbsp wholegrain breadcrumbs

4 tsp Parmesan cheese

To serve

Smashed Garlic and Lime Spud Salad (see page 190)

250g green beans, steamed

Preheat oven to 180°C/350°F/gas 4°C.

Place the haddock fillets onto a baking tray lined with parchment paper, skin side down.

Spread 1 tbsp of pesto on top of each one, then sprinkle over a tablespoon of breadcrumbs and a teaspoon of Parmesan cheese.

Bake for 15 minutes. The haddock should be white throughout.

Serve with the Garlic and Lime Spud Salad and steamed green beans on the side.

15-MINUTE
TEX-MEX WRAPS

SERVES 2 ADULTS & 2 CHILDREN

Get the little ones involved in making their own wraps. We use the 1, 2, 3 rule: 1 portion of refried beans, 2 portions of veggies and 3 portions of sauce (which is made using veggies, but we don't mention that).

For the veggie sauce
drizzle of rapeseed oil
1 red onion, roughly chopped
2 cloves garlic, crushed
2 courgettes, diced
400g (14oz) tinned tomatoes
2 tbsp tomato purée
200g (1¼ cups) cherry tomatoes, quartered
1 tsp ground cumin
1 tsp ground coriander
2 tsp sweet paprika
¾ tsp ground cinnamon
1 lime, juice only
400g (14oz) tinned black beans

For the veggies
drizzle of rapeseed oil
2 red peppers, deseeded and diced
140g (1 cup) frozen peas
140g (1 cup) frozen sweetcorn

To serve
Refried Mexican Black Beans (see page 213)
4 tortilla wraps
200ml (6oz) sour cream
4 tsp Cheddar cheese, grated

To make the sauce, heat the oil in a frying pan and gently cook the onion until it softens. Then add the garlic and cook for a further minute or two.

Add the courgette and tinned tomatoes, stirring well. Cook over a medium heat, covered, until the courgette is soft.

Add the tomato purée, cherry tomatoes, spices and lime juice, give everything a good stir, then pour into a blender and blend until the sauce is smooth and silky.

Stir in the black beans and leave aside.

Heat a little rapeseed oil in a separate frying pan, then add the peppers and cook until they are soft enough for your little ones.

Add the peas and sweetcorn, stirring well until they are cooked through.

To serve, place the sauce, veggies and refried beans on the table in separate bowls, along with the wraps and bowls of sour cream and grated cheese, and let everyone get to work making their own wraps. Messy, delicious fun!

SWEET AND SOUR CHICKPEA & NOODLE STIR-FRY

SERVES 2 ADULTS & 2 CHILDREN

When the question 'what's for dinner?' comes up in our house, this dish is usually the answer. The sauce is very quick and one of the kids' favourites too. Cut all the veggies the same size, which really helps with picky little ones.

250g (8oz) noodles
drizzle of rapeseed oil
2 red peppers, chopped
2 red onions, sliced
1 courgette, chopped
200g (7oz) long-stem broccoli
1 clove garlic, crushed
1 inch piece ginger, grated
800g (28oz) tinned chickpeas
1 tbsp maple syrup
1 tbsp sesame oil
1 tbsp soy sauce
75g (½ cup) pineapple chunks
juice 1 lime
1 tsp ground coriander
1 tsp garam masala
small handful fresh coriander, chopped, to serve

Cook the noodles according to the instructions on the packet.

Heat some rapeseed oil in a wok or frying pan until it is very hot. Add the peppers, onions, courgette and long-stem broccoli and cook until soft enough for your baby to eat. (We like ours al dente, but you will have to cook a baby's portion until softer.)

Add the garlic and ginger to the pan and cook for a minute or two more, until the garlic is cooked but not browned.

Add the chickpeas to the pan along with the maple syrup, sesame oil, soy sauce, pineapple chunks, lime juice and spices, and heat through.

Add the noodles to the pan, toss well and serve with a sprinkle of freshly chopped coriander.

AILEEN'S TIP!

For a baby-friendly dinner just press each chickpea to make them super safe for little hands.

HEALTHIER
PASTA CARBONARA

SERVES 2 ADULTS & 2 CHILDREN

This carbonara is full of flavour, and even though it doesn't use a ton of butter and cream, I promise it still tastes wonderful! Serve with a side of veggies to get that portion in there too.

400g (14oz) good quality spaghetti

2 tbsp olive oil

1 white onion, diced

1 clove garlic, crushed

125ml (½ cup) milk

125ml (½ cup) Greek yogurt

3 egg yolks

2 tbsp grated Parmesan cheese

140g (1 cup) frozen peas, cooked

small bunch fresh parsley, finely chopped, to serve

Cook the spaghetti to your liking.

Heat the oil in a saucepan, then gently fry the onion and garlic until the onion becomes translucent.

Pour in the milk and Greek yogurt and stir really well. Warm until it starts to bubble, then remove from the heat.

Whisk in the egg yolks, then sprinkle in the cheese. The sauce should be hot, which will cook the eggs perfectly.

Pour the sauce over the hot pasta, along with the peas, then sprinkle over some fresh parsley to serve.

10-MINUTE
CHICKPEA BURGERS

SERVES 2 ADULTS & 2 CHILDREN

The trick with these is to mash the chickpeas rather than blend them – it makes them much easier to form into burgers and they hold their shape better too. Easy to make and brilliant for the freezer as well.

400g (14oz) tinned chickpeas, drained

4 oat crackers

1 egg

bunch fresh coriander, finely chopped

1 large handful fresh spinach, finely chopped

zest of 1 lemon

1 tsp ground cumin

rapeseed oil, for frying

For the sauce
60ml (¼ cup) Greek yogurt

2 cloves roasted garlic, crushed

juice of ½ lime

10 mint leaves, finely chopped

ground black pepper

To serve
4 burger buns

iceberg lettuce, shredded

5 cherry tomatoes, sliced

2 spring onions, finely chopped

Place the chickpeas into a bowl. Mash with a fork until completely broken up.

Place the crackers in a pestle and mortar, grind into a fine powder, then empty into the bowl with the chickpeas.

Whisk the egg and add to the bowl with the coriander, spinach, lemon zest and cumin. Mix well, until it all comes together.

Divide the mixture into 3 equal parts, then divide one of the parts into 2. Shape into burgers – you should have 2 large and 2 small.

Heat some rapeseed oil in a frying pan, then fry the burgers until they are browned on both sides.

Make the sauce by mixing all of the ingredients until smooth and creamy.

Serve the burgers on toasted buns with a dollop of sauce, lettuce, tomato and a little spring onion.

REALLY QUICK
RAINBOW PIZZAS

SERVES 2 ADULTS & 2 CHILDREN

Sometimes how you talk about food can make a child's eyes open wide with curiosity. These colourful rainbow pizzas have plenty of veggies in them and kids love them – like, really, really love them.

4 flour tortillas

3-Ingredient Pizza Sauce (see page 230)

1 red pepper, finely chopped

1 yellow pepper, finely chopped

1 green pepper, finely chopped

70g (½ cup) sweetcorn

10 cherry tomatoes (finely chopped)

sprinkle of grated mozzarella for each one

Preheat oven to 180°C/350°F/gas 4.

Place each tortilla on a baking tray.

Add a tablespoon of pizza sauce to each one and spread with the back of a spoon.

Divide the vegetables between the tortillas.

Sprinkle with a little cheese, then bake for 12–15 minutes, until the cheese is melted and the vegetables are a little softer.

Serve warm or cold.

COCONUT POACHED SALMON
WITH MISO VEGGIES & RICE

SERVES 2 ADULTS & 2 CHILDREN

If you ask Oscar what his favourite food is, he will tell you salmon, which is fantastic because it is just so nourishing for growing kids. I always buy good quality non-farmed fish – you'll notice the difference in both colour and taste.

For the salmon
200ml (¾ cup) full fat coconut milk
4 fillets of salmon
black pepper, to season

For the vegetables
drizzle of rapeseed oil
1 red onion, finely sliced
1 inch piece root ginger, grated
2 cloves garlic, crushed
2 red peppers, finely sliced
200g (7oz) mange tout, finely sliced
300g (10oz) long-stem broccoli, finely sliced
1 tbsp miso paste
1 tbsp soy sauce
3 tbsp water
juice 1 lime

To serve
cooked brown rice
small bunch coriander, finely chopped

Add the coconut milk to a saucepan, and, while heating, use the back of a spoon to smooth it out until it is creamy.

Place the salmon fillets into the coconut milk, sprinkle over a little black pepper, then poach for about 12 minutes. When done, the salmon should be light pink throughout.

While the salmon is cooking, heat the rapeseed oil in a wok or frying pan, add the onion, ginger, garlic and vegetables and cook to your liking. You will need to cook your baby's portion for a little longer to ensure the veggies are soft enough for them to manage.

Mix the miso paste, soy sauce, water and lime juice in a bowl, then pour over the vegetables and toss.

To serve, place a portion of brown rice, some vegetables and a piece of salmon on each plate, then sprinkle over some finely chopped coriander.

 MAKE IT VEGETARIAN: Swap salmon for chickpeas and add to the veggies.

POT O' MUSSELS WITH
BREAD FOR DIPPING

SERVES 2 ADULTS & 2 CHILDREN

In my eyes, there is nothing nicer than a bowl of mussels in the middle of the table, served with artisan bread and a side of veggies. Mussels are an excellent source of iron and protein so this is a perfect dinner for little and big people. Just make sure to remove the cooked mussels from their shells for the little ones.

1kg (35oz) fresh mussels
drizzle of olive oil
1 white onion, finely diced
2 cloves garlic, crushed
2 large tomatoes, chopped
2 tsp tomato purée
1 tsp sweet paprika
60ml (¼ cup) Greek yogurt

To serve
4–5 sprigs fresh parsley, finely chopped
Crusty bread

Wash the mussels in a colander using cold water to remove any pieces of sand and dirt. Go through every mussel and remove any stringy bits that stick out. Discard mussels that are broken or stay open when you tap them on the counter.

Heat the oil in a large pot, then add the onion and cook until translucent. Add the garlic and cook for a minute until fragrant.

Add the tomatoes, tomato purée, paprika and Greek yogurt and stir well. Then add the mussels, cover with a lid, bring to the boil and cook for 4–5 minutes. Shake the saucepan to ensure they cook evenly.

Remove from the heat and pour into a large bowl. Discard any mussels that remain unopened. Sprinkle with the fresh parsley and serve with some nice crusty bread.

LOADED SPANISH
OMELETTE WITH SALAD

SERVES 2 ADULTS & 2 CHILDREN

There is something about potato and sweet fried onion in a bed of yummy egg that is just so comforting. This is a brilliant recipe to start your baby on their weaning journey as it is soft, nourishing and easy to make.

drizzle of olive oil

1 Spanish onion, finely diced

600g (21oz) baby potatoes, cooked and quartered

1 tsp smoked paprika

8 eggs

60ml (¼ cup) Greek yogurt

black pepper, to season

2 tbsp grated Parmesan

Baby Leaves with Fruit Salad (see page 203), to serve

Heat the oil in a large pan over a high heat and fry the onion until it starts to turn golden.

Add the potatoes and paprika and cook until the potatoes start to brown.

Whisk the eggs with the yogurt, pepper and cheese until smooth and creamy, then pour over the potatoes.

Turn the heat to its lowest setting and cook until the bottom starts to brown (you can check using a spatula or knife).

You can let it cook until the egg on the top has almost set and then flip over, or, if you are like me, stick the pan under the grill and cook until the top has turned golden brown and is fully set. Just be careful of plastic handles.

Cut into triangles and serve with a side of Baby Leaves with Fruit Salad.

Cook Once, Eat Twice
DINNERS

What I also call magic dinners! All of the recipes in this section make enough for two family meals – one for now and one for your freezer.

This means you can build up some handy dinners for busy days when you just can't face cooking. Plus, these dinners taste even better the second time around!

MOROCCAN
TURKEY MEATBALLS

SERVES 2 ADULTS & 2 CHILDREN

It's hard to beat these yummy turkey meatballs. This is always a winning dish!

For the meatballs
800g (28oz) turkey mince
2 medium onions, finely diced
4 cloves garlic, crushed
800g (28oz) tinned chickpeas, drained and mashed
2 tbsp rapeseed oil
30 basil leaves, finely chopped
2 lemons, zest and juice
4 tsp ground cumin
4 tsp paprika
4 tsp ground coriander
2 tsp turmeric

For the sauce
drizzle of rapeseed oil
2 onions, finely diced
2 cloves garlic, crushed
6 tbsp tomato purée
50 cherry tomatoes, quartered
2 tsp ground coriander
2 tsp ground cumin
2 tsp paprika

To serve
handful basil leaves, roughly chopped
olive oil
cooked couscous

Preheat oven to 180°C/350°F/gas 4.

Place all of the ingredients for the meatballs in a large bowl and mix well.

Divide the mixture into 30 even parts and, using your hands, roll into little balls.

Place into a baking dish, cover the dish with tin foil and bake for 20 minutes. After 20 minutes remove the foil and bake for a further 10 minutes until cooked through.

While the meatballs are cooking, make the sauce. First heat the rapeseed oil in a frying pan over a medium heat. Add the onions and gently fry until soft, then add the garlic and cook for 2–3 more minutes.

Add the tomato purée, chopped cherry tomatoes and spices and stir well. Cook for 5 minutes over a low heat, until the tomatoes are heated through.

Spoon the sauce over the meatballs, sprinkle with the basil leaves and add a light drizzle of olive oil.

Serve with warm couscous.

STICKY CHICKEN
TRAY BAKE

SERVES 2 ADULTS & 2 CHILDREN

Once you make this dish you will honestly make it again and again and again. Just use your favourite veggies and you are good to go.

8 chicken breasts, cut into bite-sized pieces

8 small sweet potatoes, peeled and cut into chunks

8 baby sweet peppers (or 2 regular-sized peppers), halved and deseeded

4 red onions, peeled and quartered

2 white onions, peeled and quartered

cloves from 2 bulbs garlic, unpeeled

For the sauce

2 small bunches fresh coriander

6 tbsp olive oil

4 ripe peaches, roughly chopped

4 tbsp maple syrup

2 tsp Dijon mustard

2 sprigs fresh rosemary, leaves picked

1 tsp ground black pepper

16 cherry tomatoes

Preheat oven to 170°C/340°F/gas 3.

Line 2 large baking trays with parchment paper – this saves a lot of cleaning afterwards.

Place the chicken, sweet potatoes, peppers, onions and garlic cloves on the trays.

To make the sauce, separate the coriander leaves from the stalks and keep aside to garnish. Place the stalks into a blender with the remaining sauce ingredients, apart from the cherry tomatoes, and blend until smooth and creamy.

Pour the sauce over the vegetables and chicken and, using your hands, make sure that everything is completely coated.

Scatter the cherry tomatoes over the mix, or if the tomatoes are still on the vine, place them on top, then bake for 45 minutes. The vegetables should all be soft if pressed between forefinger and thumb, and the chicken should be lovely and moist.

Roughly chop the reserved coriander leaves and sprinkle over to serve.

 MAKE IT VEGETARIAN: Swap chicken for a portion of chickpeas.

BABY-FRIENDLY
IRISH CHOWDER

SERVES 2 ADULTS & 2 CHILDREN

This is one of the most popular recipes on babyledfeeding.com, and for a good reason! It is hearty and comforting, creamy and delicious and, most importantly, super-healthy and quick.

splash of rapeseed oil

80g smoked fish

2 white onions, finely diced

4 cloves garlic, crushed

6 tbsp plain flour

1l (4 cups) water or fish stock

1l (4 cups) milk

4 carrots, diced

1kg (35oz) new baby potatoes, cut into chunks

8 salmon fillets (500–600g/17oz)

400g (14oz) prawns

400g (14oz) mussels, cooked and shelled (see page 136 for preparation instructions)

black pepper, to season

small bunch parsley, freshly chopped, to serve

Add the rapeseed oil to a large saucepan and heat over a medium heat.

Add the smoked fish and cook for about 5 minutes, scraping the bottom of the saucepan as you stir. This adds lovely flavour to the chowder.

Turn the heat down to low, then add the onions and garlic and cook until the onion is translucent.

Add the flour to the pot and stir really well. It is important to cook off the flour so that the chowder doesn't have a 'floury' taste.

Slowly add the fish stock or water, a little at a time, whisking constantly. This prevents the sauce from lumping. Then whisk in the milk.

Add the carrots and potatoes, then cover the pot with a lid and cook over a low–medium heat until the potatoes are almost cooked. This should take about 12–15 minutes.

Cut the salmon into chunks and add to the pot along with the prawns and give it all a good stir. Cover again and simmer for 12 minutes, then remove the lid and stir in the shelled cooked mussels.

Season with a little pepper and sprinkle with chopped parsley to serve.

ONE-PAN LEMON & GARLIC CHICKEN WITH
ASPARAGUS & BABY POTATOES

When you need a convenient dinner, one-pan meals are a lifesaver! Throw everything onto the same baking tray, place in the oven and all those yummy flavours roll into each other. This is quite garlicky, but if that's not your thing, you can reduce the amount to your own taste.

8 free-range chicken breasts

2kg (70oz) baby potatoes, quartered

4 lemons, halved

120ml (½ cup) olive oil

16 cloves garlic, skin on

4 sprigs fresh rosemary, finely chopped

2 tsp ground cumin

black pepper, to season

40 asparagus spears

AILEEN'S TIP!
For a baby-friendly dinner shred the chicken using a fork.

Preheat oven to 160°C/325°F/gas 3 and line 2 baking trays with parchment paper (this helps with the cleaning afterwards).

Place the chicken breasts on the trays and slice some crisscross lines across them.

Add the potatoes.

Squeeze the lemon halves over the chicken and place them onto the trays. As they cook they'll release more juice.

Drizzle the olive oil over the chicken and potatoes, then scatter around the garlic cloves.

Sprinkle with most of the rosemary and the cumin, season with a little pepper, then place in the oven for about 20 minutes.

Remove from the oven. Baste the chicken with the juices to keep it moist, then add the asparagus and bake for another 15 minutes, until the chicken is cooked through.

Place the chicken, potatoes and asparagus on a serving dish and cover with a little tin foil to keep warm.

Open the cloves of garlic and, using the back of a spoon, squash them until they form a paste. Stir the paste into the juices left on the tray, then pour over the chicken.

Serve with the reserved rosemary sprinkled on top.

QUINOA FALAFELS
IN A BOWL OF YUM!

SERVES 2 ADULTS & 2 CHILDREN

High in protein and iron, this dish is great for vegetarians and vegans. Get the little ones involved in making these bowls – it really helps to encourage them to eat more veg, plus it's a great way to spend an afternoon (if that's your thing).

For the falafels

drizzle of rapeseed oil

2 medium white onions, finely diced

2 cloves garlic, crushed

800g (28oz) tinned chickpeas

400g (2 cups) cooked quinoa

2 heaped tsp ground cumin

2 heaped tsp ground coriander

juice 2 lemons

4 tbsps chickpea flour (also called gram flour) or plain flour

For the tahini dressing

250ml (1 cup) Greek yogurt

125ml (½ cup) light tahini

juice 1 lemon

small bunch fresh coriander, finely chopped

For the bowls

60g (¼ cup) cooked brown rice (per bowl)

4 roasted red peppers

2 roasted courgettes

hummus (see page 229)

2 avocados, sliced

120g (4oz) feta cheese, crumbled

Preheat oven to 180°C/350°F/gas 4.

Heat the oil in a frying pan over a medium heat. Gently fry the onion until translucent, then add the garlic and cook for a minute or so more until cooked but not browned.

Add the cooked onion and garlic and the rest of the falafel ingredients to a food processor and process until the chickpeas are broken up. Be careful not to over-process, as this will make the mixture too wet.

Use an ice-cream scoop to portion the mixture out onto a baking tray lined with parchment paper. Then bake for 20 minutes until golden brown.

While the falafels are cooking, make the tahini sauce by mixing all of the ingredients together.

Serve the falafels in a bowl with a little rice, some roasted veggies, hummus and sliced avocado and a small amount of feta cheese.

CHICKEN TENDERS WITH
ROASTED VEGGIES

SERVES 2 ADULTS & 2 CHILDREN

Soft, succulent chicken, covered in seasoned breadcrumbs and served with veggie fries. If you marinate the chicken the night before, it just doesn't get better than this for a quick dinner.

8 breasts of chicken, cut into strips

500ml (2 cups) buttermilk

2 large sweet potatoes, peeled and cut into spears

2 large beetroots, peeled and cut into spears

4 large carrots, peeled and cut into spears

drizzle of rapeseed oil

For the coating

360g (4 cups) crushed crackers

2 tbsp rapeseed oil

2 tsp sweet paprika

2 tsp garlic powder

black pepper, to season

4 eggs, beaten

The night before, add the chicken to a large bowl, then pour over the buttermilk. Cover with cling film and refrigerate.

The next day, preheat oven to 180°C/350°F/gas 4. Remove the chicken from the fridge and drain.

Place the veggie spears on a tray lined with parchment paper. Drizzle over a little rapeseed oil and place into the oven. These will take a little longer than the chicken (roughly 40 minutes in total).

In a bowl, use your hands to mix the crackers, rapeseed oil, paprika, garlic powder and black pepper until totally combined.

Crack the eggs into a separate bowl and beat. Take each strip of chicken, dip it into the egg, then into the cracker mixture. Place on another baking tray lined with parchment paper.

Place the chicken into the oven and bake for 25 minutes, until cooked through.

Remove the chicken and vegetables from the oven and serve warm.

VEGGIE-LOADED
BOLOGNESE

SERVES 2 ADULTS & 2 CHILDREN

We make this dinner every single week without fail. All of the children love it (even their friends who don't like veggies). This recipe is for a double batch, but you could even make a triple batch and freeze to have on hand for busy days.

800g (28oz) good quality spaghetti

4 tbsp olive oil

2 large white onions, finely diced

4 cloves garlic, sliced

4 red peppers, diced

4 medium courgettes, diced

6 tbsp tomato purée

2 lemons, zest and juice

600g (4 cups) cherry tomatoes, halved

black pepper, to season

40 fresh basil leaves, finely chopped

Cook the spaghetti as per the pack instructions, making sure it is al dente.

Heat the olive oil in a large pot over a medium heat, then add the onion and cook for a few minutes until it becomes translucent.

Add the garlic, peppers and courgettes and cook for a few more minutes, until the vegetables start to soften slightly.

Add the tomato purée, lemon zest and juice, cherry tomatoes and pepper, then stir well. Bring the mixture to a bubble, stirring often. When the tomatoes soften and become saucy, remove from the heat.

Stir in the basil leaves, and serve over a bed of spaghetti.

GRANNY'S
FISH & BROCCOLI PIE

SERVES 2 ADULTS & 2 CHILDREN

I grew up on fish pies and this recipe is from my lovely mammy. It makes a perfect baby dish as all of the ingredients are soft and easy to manage.

rapeseed oil, for frying

2 medium white onions, finely diced

2 tbsp plain flour

500ml (2 cups) milk

500ml (2 cups) Greek yogurt

2 tsp Dijon mustard

black pepper, to season

560g (4 cups) frozen peas

2 heads broccoli, chopped into small pieces

8 fillets trout or salmon, deboned and chopped into chunks

2kg (70oz) potatoes, peeled and boiled

2 tbsp butter

small bunch fresh parsley, finely chopped

Preheat oven to 180°C/350°F/gas 4.

Heat the oil in a saucepan over a medium heat and fry the onions until they become translucent.

Add the flour and stir well. Cook for about 90 seconds, then slowly whisk in the milk, yogurt, mustard and black pepper. Stir well until the mixture starts to bubble, then remove from the heat and add the peas, broccoli and fish pieces. Give everything a good stir, then divide into 2 large casserole dishes.

Mash the potatoes with the butter and chopped parsley, then divide equally and spread over the fish mixture.

Bake in the oven for 40 minutes, until the potatoes are golden brown and the fish and veggies are cooked.

Serve warm.

CHILLI CON VEGGIE
WITH THE TRIMMINGS

SERVES 2 ADULTS & 2 CHILDREN

The best way to serve this meal is with lots of bowls on the table, letting everyone help themselves – especially babies or toddlers. When they see everyone else taking veggies with sour cream and guacamole, they will be far more inclined to try it for themselves. The guacamole and rice should be made fresh, but the chilli freezes well.

For the chilli
rapeseed oil, for frying
2 large Spanish onions, diced
4 cloves garlic, crushed
4 red peppers, finely chopped
4 courgettes, finely chopped
6 tbsp tomato purée
800g (28oz) tinned tomatoes
4 x 400g (15oz) tins red kidney beans, drained
2 tsp ground cumin
2 tsp ground coriander
4 tsp sweet paprika
1½ tsp ground cinnamon

For the guacamole (make fresh)
2 medium avocados, mashed
1 shallot, finely diced
8 cherry tomatoes, finely diced
juice 1 lime
small bunch fresh coriander, finely chopped

To serve (per meal)
200g (2 cups) cooked brown rice
200ml (¾ cup) sour cream
60g (¼ cup) Cheddar cheese, grated

Heat the oil in a pan over a medium heat. Fry the onion until golden, then add the garlic and stir well. Cook for a further minute, making sure not to brown.

Add the peppers, courgettes and tomato purée. Stir well, then pour in the tomatoes, red kidney beans and spices and stir well.

Cover with a lid and leave to simmer for about 5 minutes, then remove the lid and cook for another 5 minutes, stirring often. The vegetables should be soft enough for your little ones to manage.

To make the guacamole, simply mix all of the ingredients together in a separate bowl.

Serve the chilli over brown rice, with a big dollop of guacamole on the side, a spoonful of sour cream and a sprinkling of Cheddar cheese.

Weekend

DINNERS

You have a bit more time, the kids are all calm and you can spend time teaching them or letting them help you make the dinner.

Even still, these dinners won't take you forever. Remember, this is a family cookbook, and the only people you are trying to impress are the ones who already love you.

CHICKEN (OR TOFU)
TIKKA MASALA

SERVES 2 ADULTS & 2 CHILDREN

This is the number-one recipe on the Baby-Led Feeding website. Honestly, it has been viewed almost 500,000 times, and I have received thousands of mails from parents who have made it. Try it – you won't regret it!

1 large white onion, peeled and roughly chopped

6 cloves garlic

2 thumb-sized pieces root ginger, peeled and grated

60ml (¼ cup) rapeseed oil

1 tsp ground coriander

1 tsp ground cumin

1 tsp ground cinnamon

1 tsp garam masala

1 tsp turmeric

½ tsp mild chilli powder

400g (14oz) tinned chopped tomatoes

4 free-range chicken breasts, diced, or 250g (8oz) tofu, chopped into large cubes

4 tbsp ground almonds

2 tbsp desiccated coconut

6 heaped tbsp Greek yogurt

black pepper, to season

200g (2 cups) cooked brown rice, to serve

small bunch fresh coriander, to garnish

Add the onion, garlic, ginger and rapeseed oil to a blender. Blend until smooth, then pour into a large saucepan. Place over a medium heat and fry for about 5 minutes, until it deepens in colour.

Add all of the spices and chopped tomatoes, then give everything a good stir. Now there are two options for cooking.

Either add the chicken or tofu and sauce to a slow cooker, turn to a medium setting and cook for about 4 hours.

Or, on the hob, add the chicken or tofu to the saucepan, turn the heat to its lowest setting and simmer for 2 hours.

When the chicken is cooked and really tender, add the almonds, coconut and yogurt and season with some pepper.

Serve with brown rice and sprinkled with some fresh coriander.

YUMMY BUTTER
CHICKEN (OR TOFU)

SERVES 2 ADULTS & 2 CHILDREN

Marinate the meat the night before, then pop it into the slow cooker before you head out for the day and enjoy coming home to the delicious smell!

juice ½ lemon

250ml (1 cup) natural yogurt

1 inch piece root ginger

1 white onion, roughly chopped

2 cloves garlic

4 free-range chicken breasts, diced, or 250g (8oz) tofu, chopped into large cubes

4 tbsp tomato purée

400ml (14oz) full-fat coconut milk

1 tsp turmeric

1 tsp ground ginger

1 tsp garam masala

6 cardamom pods, crushed

black pepper, to season

To serve

200g (2 cups) cooked brown rice

small bunch fresh coriander, finely chopped

Place the lemon juice, natural yogurt, ginger, onion and garlic in a blender and blend until smooth. Pour into a bowl, add the chicken and marinate overnight.

When you are ready to cook, pour the mixture into a slow cooker or ovenproof dish. Add the remaining ingredients and stir well.

Cook in a slow cooker for about 6 hours on slow, or in an oven preheated to 140°C/275°F/gas 1, covered, for 4 hours.

Serve on a bed of brown rice with a sprinkle of fresh coriander.

RAMEN WITH
STICKY CHICKEN, BEEF OR TOFU

SERVES 2 ADULTS & 2 CHILDREN

Ramen is a mixture of soup, veggies and a protein – so use either chicken, beef or tofu. It is very nutritious and perfect for winter evenings when you are trying to get extra goodness into the entire family. Even though this looks like a lot of ingredients, it's a super-quick amazing dinner!

For the sticky chicken/beef/tofu
4 free-range chicken breasts or 250g (8oz) beef or tofu, cut into strips
1 tbsp sesame oil
1 tbsp soy sauce
1 tbsp maple syrup
4 tbsp sesame seeds

For the miso soup
60ml (¼ cup) miso paste
1 litre (4 cups) water
2 spring onions, finely sliced

For the sesame and orange carrots
2 large carrots, finely grated
drizzle of rapeseed oil
1 tsp sesame oil
juice of 1 orange
2 tbsp sesame seeds

For the grilled peppers
4 sweet peppers, sliced lengthways
2 tsp rapeseed oil

To serve
cooked buckwheat noodles
1 lime, quartered
small bunch fresh coriander, finely chopped

Place the chicken/beef/tofu, sesame oil, soy sauce and maple syrup into a bowl, stir well, then empty onto a hot frying pan. Cook for 10–15 minutes stirring often until cooked and the sauce has turned thick and sticky.

In a dry pan, sprinkle in the sesame seeds and toast until they start to pop. Scatter half over the chicken/beef/tofu and leave the others aside for the carrots.

To make the miso soup, add the miso paste to a pot, stir in the water and spring onions, then gently heat until hot but not boiling (miso should never be boiled).

To make the orange carrot, gently fry the carrot on a pan with the rapeseed and sesame oils. When soft (around 5 minutes), squeeze in the orange juice, add sesame seeds and stir well.

Lightly coat the sweet peppers in rapeseed oil, then grill on both sides until soft.

Into warm bowls, add a portion of noodles, a portion of carrots, some grilled peppers, then a ladleful of the miso soup.

Top with the sticky chicken/beef/tofu, add a wedge of lime and sprinkle with some of the fresh coriander.

HERE FISHY-FISHY
LIME, CORIANDER & GINGER SALMON POPS

SERVES 2 ADULTS & 2 CHILDREN

Kids love food on sticks and these yummy pops are a great way to load your little ones with some omega-3-rich salmon.

For the marinade

3 cloves garlic

10g (2 tsp) root ginger, peeled

80ml (¼ cup + 1 tbsp) olive oil

1 lime, zest and juice

small bunch fresh coriander

1 tsp Dijon mustard

For the skewers

400g (14oz) organic fresh salmon, cut into chunks

2 red bell peppers, cut into chunks

3 red onions, cut into chunks

2 medium-sized sweet potatoes, cooked, peeled and cut into chunks

To serve

small bunch fresh coriander, finely chopped

1 lime, quartered

Preheat oven to 170°C/340°F/gas 3.

Soak some wooden skewers for adults and lollipop sticks for babies in water.

Add all the ingredients for the marinade to a blender and blend until smooth.

Put the salmon (make sure you check for bones first) into a bowl, then add the vegetables.

Pour the marinade over the vegetables and, using your hands, coat thoroughly.

Using lollipop sticks for babies and wooden skewers for older children and adults, add a piece of salmon, pepper, onion and sweet potato, then repeat until full, with just enough free space to hold.

When you are finished, place the skewers and sticks on a tray lined with parchment paper and bake for 30 minutes, until everything is lovely and soft (make sure you can squish a pepper between your thumb and index finger before serving).

Sprinkle with fresh coriander and serve with some lime wedges.

CHICKEN AND BROCCOLI
POT PIES

SERVES 2 ADULTS & 2 CHILDREN

I am a huge fan of pies, especially on a cold winter's day. That smell of warm pastry and sauce wafting through the house makes everyone hungry. It's easy to double everything when you make this pie – then you can cook both and freeze one for another dinner during the week.

For the pastry
450g (3 cups) plain flour
220g (1 cup) butter
8 tbsp water

For the filling
1 tbsp rapeseed oil
2 medium white onions, finely chopped
3 medium carrots, finely chopped
4 free-range chicken breasts, cut into small pieces
1 clove garlic, crushed
200ml (¾ cup + 1½ tbsp) whole milk
1 heaped dessertspoon natural yogurt
80g (¼ cup) Parmesan cheese, grated
350g (12oz) tender-stem broccoli, finely chopped
1 large handful spinach, finely chopped
2 large mushrooms, finely chopped
small bunch fresh parsley, finely chopped
black pepper, to season
1 egg, beaten, for brushing

Preheat the oven to 180°C/350°F/gas 4.

To make the pastry, add the flour to a bowl, then, using your fingers, rub in the butter until it resembles fine breadcrumbs. Add the water a tablespoon at a time until the pastry comes together. Turn it out onto a well-floured work surface and roll out until it is about 0.5cm thick.

Lightly butter a 20cm pie dish, then line with the pastry and cut away the excess. Repeat, but this time use smaller ramekins for your toddler's pies. Keep the leftover pastry for the lids. Leave the pastry-lined dishes in the fridge until you are ready to fill them.

Heat the rapeseed oil in a frying pan over a medium heat and fry the onions and carrots until the carrots start to soften and the onions are translucent.

Add the chicken to the pan and cook for about 10 minutes, until the chicken is cooked through.

Add the garlic, milk, yogurt and cheese and stir well, then remove from the heat.

Add the broccoli, spinach, mushrooms and parsley and stir well. Season with some black pepper.

Divide the chicken filling between the pie dishes, then roll out the remaining pastry and cut and add a pastry lid to each one. Cut a little hole in each pie to allow air to escape. Then brush with a little beaten egg.

Bake for 30 minutes until golden.

Serve warm with a side of peas.

SPINACH GNOCCHI WITH
PESTO & VEGGIES

SERVES 2 ADULTS & 2 CHILDREN

This is fuel for superhero kids, packed full of green goodness and super-tasty too. Oscar honestly believes that when he eats this his muscles grow humongous!

For the gnocchi

1 tsp olive oil

3 large handfuls fresh spinach

450g (2 cups) cold mashed potato

150g (1 cup) plain flour

1 egg, beaten

black pepper, to season

2 tbsp Parmesan cheese

drizzle of rapeseed oil, for frying

2 red peppers, sliced

150g (8oz) green beans, cut into small pieces

60ml (¼ cup) Easy-Peasy Basil & Spinach Pesto (see page 220)

basil leaves, to serve

Heat the olive oil in a pan, add the spinach and stir continuously until wilted. Leave aside to cool fully. When cold, squeeze the liquid out of the spinach, finely chop and add to a bowl with the potato, flour, egg, pepper and Parmesan cheese. Mix until fully combined.

Turn onto a well-floured surface, then roll into long log shapes, roughly 2cm thick. Cut into 3cm pieces, then use the back of a fork to mark each one.

Half-fill a saucepan with water and bring to the boil. Add the gnocchi in batches and cook each batch for about 3 minutes – they're cooked when they rise to the surface. Using a slotted spoon, remove from the water and leave aside until they're all ready.

Heat the rapeseed oil in a pan, and gently fry the peppers and green beans until soft enough for your little ones to manage. Add the gnocchi and pesto to the pan and stir. Heat through, then serve with a sprig of basil on top of each portion.

AILEEN'S TIP!

Gnocchi can be cooked from frozen. Just pop into a pot of boiling water. It is cooked when it floats to the surface.

STUFFED PEPPERS WITH
SWEET POTATO FRIES

SERVES 2 ADULTS & 2 CHILDREN

These sweet, delicious baby peppers are stuffed with minced beef and veggies, but you can also replace the meat with beans for a high-protein vegetarian meal. I use mini peppers for my toddler, as they are much more appropriate to his size.

2 large sweet potatoes, cut into spears
drizzle of rapeseed oil, for baking
4 red bell peppers
4 mini sweet peppers, halved lengthways
olive oil, for roasting and frying
1 medium white onion, finely diced
2 cloves garlic
400g (14oz) minced beef or 800g (28oz) tinned black beans
400g (14oz) tinned tomatoes
2 tbsp tomato purée
juice 1 lemon
4 tbsp Parmesan cheese
400g (2 cups) cooked brown rice
20 basil leaves, finely chopped
100g mozzarella cheese

Preheat oven to 180°C/350°F/gas 4.

Drizzle the sweet potatoes with a little rapeseed oil, then bake for about 40 minutes, until cooked through.

While the sweet potatoes are cooking, line a baking tray with parchment paper. Cut the tops off the bell peppers, straight under the stem, keeping the tops for lids. Remove the seeds from the bell peppers and the sweet pepper halves, then rub each one with a little olive oil to evenly coat. Place the peppers (and lids) on the tray, making sure the bell peppers stand up, and bake for 15 minutes. Remove from the oven and leave aside.

Heat a little olive oil in a saucepan over a medium heat. Fry the onion until translucent, then add the garlic and beef and cook until the beef has browned. If using beans instead, add now.

Add the tomatoes, tomato purée, lemon juice and Parmesan, stir well and simmer until the mixture starts to thicken.

Add the rice to the pot, along with the basil leaves, and stir well.

Fill the peppers with the filling, break apart the mozzarella and divide between the peppers.

Return to the oven and bake for another 15 minutes, until the cheese has melted and the peppers are cooked.

Serve the peppers with a side of the sweet potato fries.

 MAKE IT VEGETARIAN: Swap beef for black beans.

HOMEMADE FISH GOUJONS WITH
MUSHY PEAS & OVEN CHIPS

SERVES 2 ADULTS & 2 CHILDREN

Making your own fish goujons is super-easy and the best part is that they freeze really well, just like the store-bought kind – except they taste way nicer, of course.

500g (17oz) potatoes, washed and cut into chips (I leave the skins on)

rapeseed oil

1 tsp paprika

750g (26oz) fresh hake fillet, skinned and deboned

1 lemon, juice and zest

black pepper, to season

100g plain flour

2 eggs, beaten

4 slices wholegrain breadcrumbs

Mammy's Mushy Peas (see page 200), to serve

Preheat oven to 180°C/350°F/gas 4. Line a tray with parchment paper.

Add the sweet potatoes, a drizzle of rapeseed oil and the paprika to a bowl and toss well to coat. Spread on the baking tray and bake until soft and tender, about 25 minutes.

Place the hake, lemon juice and zest and some pepper in a food processor and process until the fish has broken up. Turn out into a small tray lined with cling film and firmly press down with a spatula. Cut into finger-sized portions. Place in the fridge for about an hour to make it a little easier to handle.

Gently remove each finger. Dip first into the flour, then into the egg and finally coat with breadcrumbs (you can freeze them at this point if you want to plan ahead for future dinners).

Heat a little rapeseed oil in a frying pan over a medium heat, then fry the fish goujons until golden brown on both sides.

Serve the fish goujons with the sweet potatoes fries and a side of warm mushy peas.

WHATEVER'S IN THE FRIDGE DINNER
HUMMUS, ROASTED VEGGIES, PITTAS & YOGURT DIP

SERVES 2 ADULTS & 2 CHILDREN

You know when you open a cookbook and think 'I want to make this', but then realise you don't have the ingredients? Well, this is the recipe for you. Just use whatever veggies you have lying around if you don't have the ones used here.

For the roasted veggies

2 red peppers, deseeded and sliced

1 aubergine, cut into large dice

2 courgettes, cut into large dice

2 red onions, peeled and cut into large dice

drizzle of olive oil

For the hummus

400g (14oz) tinned chickpeas drained

4 tbsp tahini

4 tbsp lemon juice

4 tbsp olive oil

½ clove garlic (or 3 cloves roasted garlic)

½ tsp paprika

4 tbsp water

black pepper, to season

250g (1 cup) any puréed veg – e.g. roasted beetroot, roasted sweet potato, steamed broccoli, raw spinach, raw kale, roasted carrot

For the yogurt sauce

250ml (1 cup) Greek yogurt

½ medium cucumber, grated

½ clove garlic or 3 cloves roasted garlic, crushed

juice ½ lemon

black pepper, to season

3 warm wholemeal pitta breads or flatbreads, to serve

Preheat oven to 180°C/350°F/gas 4.

Place the veggies onto a baking tray, drizzle with a little olive oil, then roast until soft (around 40 minutes).

While the vegetables are roasting, make the hummus by adding all of the ingredients to a food processor and processing until smooth and creamy. You can add a little extra water, one spoon at a time, to get the consistency you want.

To make the yogurt sauce, simply add all of the ingredients to a bowl and stir well.

To serve, line the inside of each pitta with a good dollop of hummus, spread evenly with the back of a spoon. Add a helping of veggies, then top with the yogurt sauce. Serve a whole one per adult and a half per child.

FAJITAS WITH
PULLED BEEF & VEGGIES

SERVES 2 ADULTS & 2 CHILDREN

This is a great dinner to make when you have people coming over. It is easy to prepare and cooks gently in the oven or slow cooker until the beef is super-tender. It's perfect for little ones, as it is easy for them to manage.

For the pulled beef
rapeseed oil, for frying
1 medium onion, finely diced
black pepper, to season
1 tsp ground cumin
1 tsp ground coriander
2 tsp sweet paprika
¾ tsp ground cinnamon
juice 1 lime
400g (14oz) tinned tomatoes
2 tbsp tomato purée
1½ kg (52oz) rib of beef
1 medium red onion, finely diced
2 red peppers, diced
2 courgettes, diced

To serve
8 soft-shell tacos (3 per adult, 1 per child), warmed
1 avocado, sliced
60g (¼ cup) Cheddar cheese, grated
100ml (½ cup) sour cream

Heat the rapeseed oil in your slow-cooker pot over a medium heat or in a saucepan on the hob. Add the onion and fry until it becomes translucent. Add the pepper, spices, lime juice, tomatoes and tomato purée and give everything a good stir.

If cooking in the oven, preheat to 140°C/275°F/gas 1. Transfer the tomato sauce to a roasting tin and place the beef on top. Cover with tin foil and cook for 3 hours, then remove and cook for a further hour uncovered. Baste every 40 minutes or so to keep it really tender.

If using a slow cooker, place the rib of beef on top of the sauce and spoon some sauce over it. Cook for around 6 hours on a medium setting without removing the lid.

About 10 minutes before you are ready to serve, heat a little rapeseed oil in a frying pan, then fry all of the vegetables until they are tender enough for little hands.

Shred the beef using 2 forks until easy for little hands to manage.

To assemble the tacos, place a warm soft-shell taco onto a plate, add a little of the pulled beef, followed by some veggies, and top with avocado, a sprinkle of cheese and a dollop of sour cream.

HIDDEN VEGGIE
MAC & CHEESE

SERVES 2 ADULTS & 2 CHILDREN

This is an update of the mac and cheese muffins from my first book, only this time I have loaded it with hidden veggies. Great for those days when your little ones are being fussy and you just want to get some goodness into them.

260g (9oz) macaroni pasta

2 large carrots, cut into chunks

½ large head cauliflower, cut into chunks

½ butternut squash, cut into chunks

500ml (2 cups) milk, plus 60ml (1/4 cup) extra for the sauce

50g (1¾ oz) unsalted butter

2 tbsp flour

125g (1 cup) Cheddar cheese, grated

½ tsp ground nutmeg

black pepper, to season

1 slice wholemeal bread, blitzed into crumbs

Cook the pasta according to the instructions on the pack. When it is al dente, drain and leave aside.

Add all of the vegetables to a steamer over a pot of boiling water and gently steam for about 10 minutes, until the vegetables are soft but with a little bite.

Place the vegetables in a blender with 500ml milk until smooth and really creamy.

Melt the butter in a saucepan over a low heat, then whisk in the flour and stir well until it forms a roux (or paste). Whisk in 60ml milk, until the sauce is smooth, then pour in the puréed vegetables and mix really well.

Bring to a bubble, remove from the heat and stir in the cheese, nutmeg, pepper and cooked pasta.

Place the breadcrumbs into a dry pan and toast until crunchy.

Serve the mac and cheese in bowls with a sprinkling of toasted breadcrumbs on top.

TURKEY BURGERS &
SWEET POTATO FRIES

SERVES 2 ADULTS & 2 CHILDREN

This is one of our favourite weekend dinners. You could easily make a triple batch and freeze the extras for those crazy, busy days you don't feel like cooking!

2 large sweet potatoes, cut into spears
rapeseed oil, for frying

For the burgers
400g (14oz) free-range turkey, minced
1 egg
60g (1 cup) breadcrumbs
1 tsp ground cumin
1 tsp sweet paprika
1 clove garlic, crushed
1 tbsp grated root ginger
black pepper, to season

To serve
2 large and 2 small burger buns
8 cherry tomatoes, thinly sliced
5 leaves iceberg lettuce, shredded
1 sweet white onion, finely sliced
Egg-Free Aioli (see page 231)

Preheat oven to 180°C/350°F/gas 4.

Place the sweet potatoes on a baking tray lined with parchment paper. Drizzle with a little rapeseed oil, then roast for 35 minutes, until the spears are soft and cooked through.

While the potatoes are cooking, make the burgers by adding all of the ingredients to a large bowl and, using your hands, mixing well.

Divide the meat into 3 equal parts. Shape 2 parts into large burgers for the adults. Divide the last part into two and shape into burgers for the children.

To serve, lightly toast the buns and place a burger on top of each. Garnish with tomato, lettuce, onion and aioli. Serve with the softly roasted sweet potato fries.

On The
SIDE

Chicken is great, and we'd never say no to a good veggie burger, but what really makes dinner special is the addition of a few great side dishes. From roasted sweet potato fries to Mammy's Mushy Peas, there's something here for everyone.

You can also use side dishes to make a yummy tapas-style dinner that kids really, really love. It's a brilliant way for them to try new tastes – and, more importantly, veggies!

In this section you will find:

A Side of Potatoes

A Side of Vegetables

A Side of Quirkyness

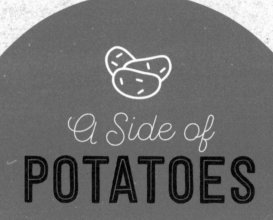

A Side of
POTATOES

We are an Irish family so spuds come with the territory. Potatoes are a great addition to any meal – they are really filling and high in potassium and vitamin C.

While potatoes are classed as a vegetable, they don't count towards your five a day (although sweet potatoes do). So it is important to make sure your little ones don't fill up too much on the humble spud to ensure they get adequate vitamins from other veggies. I normally give my toddler a baby potato, some meat or beans and veggies on the side to ensure he is getting everything he needs. He gets more potatoes when the veggies are demolished!

POTATO
ROSTI

SERVES 2 ADULTS & 2 CHILDREN

When I was around 8 years old, my dad came home from work one day and said he was going to show me how to make 'boxty', a dish his mother had made him when he was a little boy. This recipe always reminds me of that night – I just hope my dad thinks it's up to standard.

4 large potatoes, peeled

1 medium white onion, finely diced

black pepper, to season

1 large egg, beaten

1 bunch fresh parsley, finely chopped

drizzle of rapeseed oil, for frying

Grate the potatoes, then place in a clean tea towel and squeeze out the moisture.

Add the potatoes to a bowl with the onion, pepper, egg and parsley, then stir until the mixture is fully combined.

Heat the rapeseed oil in a frying pan, then turn the heat down to medium. Add an ice-cream scoop of the potato mixture to the pan. Press down with a spatula to flatten into a pancake shape.

Fry on both sides until golden brown.

Keep warm in the oven until all the mixture has been used up.

Serve warm with another sprinkle of black pepper (and a sprinkle of salt for the grown-ups).

ASIAN-SPICED
BABY SPUDS

SERVES 2 ADULTS & 2 CHILDREN

This is a really delicious side, especially with curry! My kids also love these cold, so they are great for picnics or school lunches.

4 tbsp rapeseed oil

2 tsp ground cumin

1 tsp cumin seeds
(or another tsp ground cumin)

1 tbsp ground coriander

1 tsp ground turmeric

1 whole ripe mango,
peeled and diced

1kg (2 lbs) baby potatoes,
boiled and halved

small bunch coriander leaves,
to serve

Preheat oven to 180°C/350°F/gas 4.

Place the rapeseed oil, cumin, cumin seeds, coriander, turmeric and mango in a bowl and mix well.

Put the baby potatoes on a baking tray lined with parchment paper and pour the oil and spice mix over them.

Use a spatula to coat the potatoes (you can use your hands but the turmeric will turn them yellow!).

Bake in the oven for 30 minutes or until the potatoes have become crispy and golden brown.

Remove from the oven and place into a large serving bowl. Scatter over the coriander leaves to serve.

HOME
FRIES

SERVES 2 ADULTS & 2 CHILDREN

When I lived in San Francisco, home fries were one of my favourite things when I ate out for breakfast – not healthy, but so tasty. This recipe, however, is my healthy version. A yummy way of eating leftover potatoes.

2 tbsp rapeseed oil

1 medium white onion, finely diced

1 clove garlic, crushed

4 large leftover potatoes (skins on), cut into 1 inch dice

2 stalks fresh thyme, leaves finely chopped

black pepper, to season

1 tbsp apple cider vinegar

bunch fresh coriander, finely chopped, to serve

Heat 1 tablespoon of oil in a frying pan over a medium heat, then fry the onion until it starts to turn golden. Add the garlic and cook for a further minute, then remove and place into a bowl for later.

Heat the other tablespoon of oil in the pan, and when smoking hot add the chopped potatoes.

Let the potatoes cook on the pan untouched until golden on the bottom, then use a spatula to turn them and repeat until golden all over. You may have to do them in batches.

Return the onions and garlic to the pan, along with the chopped thyme leaves, pepper and vinegar. Stir really well and cook for a further minute or two, until the onions start to stick to the potatoes.

Pour into a serving bowl and scatter some finely chopped coriander on top.

BAKED VEGGIE-LOADED
BABY POTATOES

MAKES ABOUT 24

This is a really easy recipe that will have your children eating lots of veggies. It's as easy to make a double batch as it is to make one, and they freeze really well.

1kg (2lbs) baby potatoes
rapeseed oil, for frying
1 medium white onion, finely diced
2 cloves garlic, crushed
½ head broccoli, steamed
½ head cauliflower, steamed
60ml (¼ cup) milk
1 tbsp butter
140g (1 cup) frozen peas
handful fresh parsley, finely chopped
black pepper, to season
sprinkle of Cheddar cheese, grated, for each one

Preheat oven to 200°C/400°F/gas 6.

Prick the baby potatoes with a fork before placing on an oven tray and baking for about 40 minutes (or until soft).

Allow the cooked potatoes to cool fully. Then cut them in half lengthways and scoop the soft potato into a bowl, leaving the skins aside for later.

Heat a little rapeseed oil in a pan, then add the onion and fry until it starts to become translucent. Add the garlic and cook for another minute until soft but not browning, then spoon the onion and garlic into the potato mixture.

Add the steamed broccoli and cauliflower, milk and butter. Use a potato masher to mash until smooth.

Stir in the peas and parsley and season with a little pepper. Divide the mixture between the potato skins, then sprinkle a little Cheddar cheese on top of each one.

Bake for 25–30 minutes until golden.

Serve warm or cold.

SMASHED GARLIC
AND LIME SPUD SALAD

SERVES 4 ADULTS & 4 CHILDREN

A good potato salad is a great thing to bring to any party, and this one goes down a treat with everyone, especially the kids.

6 large potatoes, cut into bite-sized chunks

4 tbsp rapeseed or olive oil

1 bulb garlic

250ml (1 cup) Greek yogurt

1 tsp Dijon mustard

3 spring onions, finely sliced

1 tbsp apple cider vinegar

1 tsp turmeric

1 tbsp cumin seeds

juice 2 limes

small bunch fresh coriander, finely chopped

Preheat oven to 200°C/400°F/gas 6.

Place the potatoes on a baking tray lined with parchment paper and drizzle them with the oil. Wrap the whole bulb of garlic in foil and place on the tray too.

Roast the potatoes and garlic for around 30 minutes, until cooked through, then remove from the oven and leave to cool fully. The garlic cloves should be soft and cooked through.

Place the Greek yogurt, Dijon mustard, spring onions, vinegar, turmeric, cumin seeds and lime juice in a bowl and stir until smooth and creamy.

Remove the garlic cloves from their skins, squish with your fingers, then place into a bowl with the cooled potatoes.

Spoon the sauce over, stir really well, then sprinkle the coriander on top.

Keep in the fridge until ready to serve.

SWEET POTATO
GROW-QUETTES

MAKES 24

Croquettes were a side we normally had only at Christmas. That was until I made this recipe. I call these grow-quettes because they are full of good ingredients that help little kids grow super-strong. They're great for lunches too!

1 large sweet potato, peeled and roasted

2 carrots, chopped and steamed

¼ head (1 cup) steamed broccoli, finely chopped

2 large handfuls spinach, finely chopped

1 clove garlic, crushed

1 tbsp rapeseed oil

small bunch parsley, finely chopped

60g (½ cup) grated Cheddar cheese

1 egg

For the crumb

1 egg, beaten

100g (2 cups) breadcrumbs

Preheat oven to 180°C/350°F/gas 4.

Place the sweet potato, carrots and broccoli in a bowl and use a potato masher or fork to mash until smooth.

Add the spinach, garlic, rapeseed oil, parsley, cheese and egg.

Using a wooden spoon, mix well until fully combined.

Take an ice-cream scoop of the mixture and form into a croquette shape.

Dip each croquette into the beaten egg, then roll in the breadcrumbs.

Place on a baking tray lined with parchment paper and bake for 25 minutes, until golden.

Serve warm or cold.

SWEET POTATO FRIES WITH
2-MINUTE GARLIC DIP

SERVES 2 ADULTS & 2 CHILDREN

I have been trying for ages to make sweet potato fries that turn out crispy, just like you get them in restaurants. The trick is semolina flour and double baking. These are amazing and go with everything!

2 large sweet potatoes, peeled and cut into chips

3 tbsp rapeseed oil

35g (¼ cup) semolina flour

1 tbsp onion powder

1 tbsp garlic powder

black pepper, to season

For the dip

125ml (½ cup) sour cream

½ clove garlic, crushed

small bunch fresh coriander, finely chopped, plus extra for garnish

juice ½ lime

Preheat oven to 180°C/350°F/gas 4.

Place the sweet potatoes on a baking tray, drizzle with the oil and bake for 20 minutes, until soft.

Remove from the oven, sprinkle with the semolina, onion powder, garlic powder and some black pepper.

Use a spatula to toss the sweet potatoes in the coating, then return to the oven for another 20 minutes, until golden and crispy.

Make the sauce by adding all of the ingredients to a bowl and stirring really well.

Serve the fries with the dip on the side and sprinkled with a little extra coriander.

A Side of
VEGGIES

Getting your children to eat and enjoy
veggies is a long-term goal. It may not
happen straight away, but it helps to
make veggies fun and,
most importantly, tasty!

ROASTED
CAULIFLOWER WITH GOAT'S CHEESE

SERVES 2 ADULTS & 2 CHILDREN

My kids were not huge fans of cauliflower until I started cooking it like this.
This recipe is so easy and is a perfect side for Sunday dinner.

1 large head cauliflower, cut into florets

60ml (¼ cup) olive oil

black pepper, to season

60g (½ cup) goat's cheese

2 tsp garlic powder

2 tsp onion powder

2 tsp sweet paprika

1 tbsp apple cider vinegar

small bunch fresh parsley, finely chopped, to serve

Preheat oven to 180°C/350°F/gas 4.

Place the cauliflower on a baking tray lined with parchment paper.

Add the oil, pepper, goat's cheese, garlic and onion powders, paprika and apple cider vinegar to a blender and blend until smooth.

Pour the sauce over the cauliflower, then use your hands to toss until fully coated.

Roast in the oven for 25 minutes, tossing halfway through, until the cauliflower is cooked and a lovely golden colour.

Scatter the parsley on top to serve.

ROASTED
BROCCOLI

SERVES 2 ADULTS & 2 CHILDREN

I seem to be the last person to get into roasted broccoli. Now that I've made it, I am totally addicted.

1 large head broccoli, cut into small florets

60ml (¼ cup) rapeseed or olive oil

1 clove garlic, crushed

1 lemon, juice and zest

black pepper, to season

2 tbsp balsamic vinegar

Preheat oven to 180°C/350°F/gas 4.

Place the broccoli on a baking tray lined with parchment paper.

Add the oil, garlic, lemon juice and zest, pepper and balsamic vinegar to a bowl and stir well.

Pour the sauce over the broccoli and use your hands to coat thoroughly.

Roast in the oven for 15 minutes, then use a tongs to turn each piece over. Return to the oven and cook for a further 10 minutes.

Serve warm.

SWEET
ORANGE CARROTS

SERVES 2 ADULTS & 2 CHILDREN

The sauce for this is amazing and can be used in many things, from sticky chicken to sticky tofu to stir-fried vegetables.

500g (4 cups) baby carrots, halved lengthways

1 orange, juice and zest

1 thumb-sized piece root ginger, grated

1 tbsp maple syrup

1 tbsp sesame oil

1 tbsp soy sauce

To serve

small bunch fresh coriander, finely chopped

40g (¼ cup) almonds, crushed

Preheat oven to 180°C/350°F/gas 4.

Place the carrots on a baking tray lined with parchment paper.

Add the orange juice and zest, ginger, maple syrup, sesame oil and soy sauce to a bowl and whisk until combined.

Pour over the carrots, then roast for 20 minutes. Use a spatula to flip them over, and roast for a further 20 minutes, until soft.

Scatter the coriander and crushed almonds on top.

MAMMY'S
MUSHY PEAS

SERVES 2 ADULTS & 2 CHILDREN

These are not like the mushy peas you had as a child – they are more like mashed fresh peas, with a whole lot of flavour. We love them with fish goujons and wedges or with mashed potato and roast chicken.

420g (3 cups) frozen peas, defrosted

2 cloves garlic, crushed

juice ½ lemon

10 mint leaves

2 tbsp olive oil

black pepper, to season

1 tbsp grated Parmesan

2 tbsp water

Place all of the ingredients into a food processor and pulse a few times until the peas have totally broken up and become more like a paste.

Add to a pot over a medium heat. Once the peas start to warm up, turn the heat to a simmer and stir constantly for about 5 minutes, until the peas are really fragrant and the garlic tastes cooked.

Serve warm.

CARROT AND APPLE
SALAD

SERVES 2 ADULTS & 2 CHILDREN

If you are looking for a way to get your little ones eating raw carrot, this is it! A yummy and super-simple salad that goes down a treat with a baked potato or as a side to any meal.

2 carrots, finely grated
2 apples, finely grated
2 tbsp sesame seeds
40g (¼ cup) raisins
juice and zest ½ orange
juice ½ lemon
3 tbsp extra virgin olive oil
1 tbsp apple cider vinegar
pinch black pepper

Place the carrots, apples, sesame seeds and raisins in a bowl.

Whisk together the remaining ingredients, then drizzle over the carrot and apple mixture.

Toss the salad until fully coated, then serve.

BABY LEAVES WITH FRUIT SALAD

SERVES 2 ADULTS & 2 CHILDREN

A tip that worked well to get my kids eating salad is to chop everything up into really teeny, tiny pieces and always add fruit they love. Fruit makes bitter leaves taste sweet and kids love sweet!

3 large handfuls baby leaves, finely chopped

2 spring onions, finely chopped

12 cherry tomatoes, finely chopped

1 carrot, grated

1 beetroot, grated

12 red grapes

8 strawberries

juice ½ lime

1 tbsp good quality sweet balsamic vinegar

1 tbsp extra virgin olive oil

30g (¼ cup) goat's cheese

35g (¼ cup) sunflower seeds

Place all the fruit and vegetables into a bowl.

Add the lime juice, vinegar and olive oil to another bowl and mix well. Drizzle over the salad, then toss.

Crumble the goat's cheese on top and mix well.

Heat a dry pan over a medium heat, add the sunflower seeds and stir until they start to turn golden. Sprinkle over the salad then serve. (For smaller babies with no teeth, crush seeds first using a pestle and mortar.)

BEAN AND VEGGIE
SALAD

SERVES 2 ADULTS & 2 CHILDREN

This is a great side for barbecues and parties, or make when you want to add a whole lot of colour to your dinner plate.

400g (15oz) tinned kidney beans, drained

400g (15oz) tinned black beans, drained

400g (15oz) tinned butter beans, drained

70g (½ cup) frozen peas, cooked

70g (½ cup) sweetcorn

1 sweet red onion, finely diced

1 red bell pepper, finely diced

large bunch fresh coriander, finely chopped

1 mango, peeled and diced

For the sauce

60ml (¼ cup) balsamic vinegar

60ml (¼ cup) extra virgin olive oil

2 tbsp maple syrup

juice 1 lime

½ tsp ground cumin

½ tsp ground coriander

Place the beans, vegetables and mango in a bowl.

Heat a pot over a high heat, then add all of the sauce ingredients. When it starts to bubble, turn the heat to a simmer and cook for about 10 minutes, stirring regularly, until the sauce starts to thicken slightly.

Pour the sauce over the beans and veggies and stir well to combine.

Cover the bowl and refrigerate for at least 2 hours before serving.

HEALTHY
CAULIFLOWER GRATIN

SERVES 2 ADULTS & 2 CHILDREN

This is a great side for any dinner. Cauliflower in a cheese sauce that is also healthy and contains a whole portion of veggies? Yes, please!

1 large head cauliflower, cut into florets

375ml (1½ cups) milk

½ white onion

3 tbsp butter

3 tbsp flour

60g (½ cup) Cheddar cheese, plus 2 tbsp for sprinkling on top

black pepper, to season

bunch fresh parsley, finely chopped

Place the cauliflower in an ovenproof dish.

Pour the milk into a blender with the onion, then blend until smooth.

Melt the butter in a saucepan over a low heat, then stir in the flour to make a roux. Cook the flour for about 1 minute, stirring constantly.

Whisk in the milk and onion mixture really slowly, stirring continuously to prevent lumps. Allow the sauce to thicken, then cook for about 2 minutes, making sure to keep stirring so it doesn't stick to the pot.

Sprinkle in the cheese, season with pepper, then add the parsley and stir well until the cheese is fully melted.

Pour the sauce over the cauliflower and toss until fully covered. Sprinkle the remaining 2 tablespoons of cheese on top.

Cover the dish with foil and bake for 30 minutes, then remove the foil and bake for a further 15 minutes, until the cheese has turned golden.

A Side of
QUIRKYNESS

These are great additions to your family meals. Grains and seeds are an essential part of a healthy diet, and you'll have no trouble getting your little ones to eat any of these dishes.

RISOTTO WITH
GOAT'S CHEESE & PEAS

SERVES 2 ADULTS & 2 CHILDREN

I used to think risotto took way too much time. But it is actually a pretty quick meal to cook and is so soft and easy for little hands to manage. Yes, it's messy for babies but it's full of goodness!

3 tbsp olive oil

2 shallots or 1 small white onion, finely diced

2 cloves garlic, crushed

280g (2 cups) frozen peas

280g (2 cups) risotto rice

1¼ litres (4½ cups) vegetable or chicken stock, heated

200g (8oz) good quality goat's cheese

½ head broccoli, steamed

small bunch parsley, finely chopped

Heat the oil over a medium heat, then add the shallots or onion. Cook until translucent, then add the garlic and peas and cook for a further minute.

Add the risotto rice with a ladleful of the heated stock and stir until the liquid has been fully absorbed.

Add another ladleful of stock and stir well until it has been absorbed too. Repeat until the stock has been used up and the rice is creamy and tender.

Crumble in the goat's cheese and steamed broccoli and mix well.

Serve with a sprinkle of parsley.

THE LOVELIEST
BULGUR WHEAT SALAD

SERVES 2 ADULTS & 2 CHILDREN

Bulgur wheat is inexpensive, nourishing and easy to prepare. You will always find this dish in my picnic basket because my kids love it and it has plenty of veggies in it too.

1 butternut squash, diced
2 medium beetroot, diced
2 medium carrots, diced
2 tbsp rapeseed oil
2 tbsp maple syrup
225g (1 cup) bulgur wheat
500ml (2 cups) water or stock

For the dressing
60ml (¼ cup) extra virgin olive oil
juice ½ lemon
10 basil leaves
35g (¼ cup) pine nuts
1 tsp ground coriander
2 tbsp parsley, finely chopped

seeds of 1 pomegranate, to decorate

Preheat oven to 180°C/350°F/gas 4.

Place the vegetables on a tray lined with parchment paper. Drizzle the rapeseed oil and maple syrup over, then toss well.

Roast in the oven for 30 minutes, until the vegetables are soft, tossing halfway through. Allow to cool fully.

Add the bulgur wheat and water to a pot, stir well, bring to the boil, then cover and simmer for about 12 minutes until tender. Drain off any liquid, then leave aside to cool fully.

Make the dressing by adding all of the ingredients to a blender and blending until smooth.

To assemble, place the vegetables and bulgur wheat in a bowl, drizzle the dressing over, then use a spoon to stir well until everything is fully coated.

Decorate with pomegranate seeds and serve.

MANGO & LIME
QUINOA

SERVES 2 ADULTS & 2 CHILDREN

Quinoa is an amazing food. It is high in protein so we eat it a lot at home, now that half my family is vegetarian. For smaller babies, roast the pepper before adding to make sure it is soft enough for them to eat.

190g (1 cup) quinoa
500ml (2 cups) water
1 red bell pepper, diced
1 mango, peeled and diced
140g (1 cup) peas, cooked
2 spring onions, finely diced

For the dressing
juice and zest 1 lemon
1 tbsp olive oil
2 tsp apple cider vinegar
small bunch fresh coriander
½ tsp cumin
½ tsp coriander
½ tsp turmeric

To cook the quinoa, first place it in a sieve, then run under the cold tap until the water runs clear. Then place the quinoa and water in a medium saucepan. Bring to the boil, stirring occasionally, then reduce heat to low, cover the pot with a lid and simmer for about 15 minutes, until the water has been completely absorbed.

In a serving bowl, place the bell pepper, mango, peas and spring onions.

To make the dressing, whisk all of the ingredients together until fully blended.

Toss the quinoa, vegetables and mango in the dressing.

Serve warm or cold.

REFRIED
MEXICAN BLACK BEANS

SERVES 2 ADULTS & 2 CHILDREN

This is the easiest and tastiest way to eat refried beans. You can cook them in less than 10 minutes and they freeze really well, so make double or even triple – they will always come in handy.

1 tbsp rapeseed oil
1 medium onion, very finely diced
2 cloves garlic, crushed
800g (29oz) tinned black beans, drained
1 tsp paprika
3 tbsp olive oil
juice ½ lime
black pepper, to season

Heat the rapeseed oil in a pan over a medium heat, then add the onion and fry until starting to turn golden brown, normally 8–10 minutes.

Add the garlic, beans, paprika, olive oil and lime juice and season with pepper. Stir well and cook for 3–4 minutes, stirring continuously, to thoroughly cook the garlic.

Use a stick blender or normal blender to blend until really smooth and creamy.

Serve over a warm tortilla with salsa.

BEAN & VEGGIE
BAKE BITES

SERVES 2 ADULTS & 2 CHILDREN

This was one of the first dishes I ever made for Oscar, when he was only six months old, and it was a winner with the entire family. Great for days when you want something from the freezer quick!

2 tbsp rapeseed oil

1 Spanish onion, finely diced

2 cloves garlic, crushed

400g (15oz) tinned kidney beans, drained

400g (15oz) tinned black beans, drained

400g (15oz) tinned butter beans, drained

140g (1 cup) sweetcorn

140g (1 cup) peas

1 red bell pepper, finely diced

1 medium courgette, finely diced

1 tsp ground cumin

3 stalks fresh parsley, finely chopped

8 eggs

Preheat oven to 180°C/350°F/gas 4.

Heat the rapeseed oil in a frying pan over a medium heat, then fry the onion until golden (about 8 minutes). Add the garlic and cook for a further 2 minutes, stirring continuously.

Add the beans, corn, peas, pepper, courgette and cumin. Cook until the courgette starts to soften, then remove from the heat and sprinkle in the parsley.

In a large bowl, whisk the eggs until light and fluffy, then add the bean and vegetable mixture. Stir until fully combined.

Line a baking tray with parchment paper, then pour in the egg and bean mixture. Use the back of a spoon to smooth the top down until flat.

Bake for 25 minutes until set.

Slice into about 16 squares and serve.

THE WORLD'S
BEST STUFFING BALLS*

SERVES 2 ADULTS & 2 CHILDREN

Stuffing is just like puppies: it's not just for Christmas! Although, my kids say that these stuffing balls are their favourite part of the Christmas dinner. I have always said I would pass this recipe on to them, so I'm doing that by including it here.

10 slices wholemeal bread

10 tortilla chips

135g (1 cup) hazelnuts or 4 extra slices of bread

1 medium sweet white onion, quartered

3 leaves fresh sage

small bunch fresh parsley

pepper, to season

60g (¼ cup) butter, melted

Preheat oven to 180°C/350°F/gas 4.

Place the bread, tortilla chips and hazelnuts in a food processor and pulse into fine crumbs.

Add the onion, sage, parsley and pepper, then pulse until the mixture comes together and has totally broken up.

Pour in the butter and pulse for a few seconds.

Form into balls and place on a baking tray lined with parchment paper.

Cook for 20 minutes until crispy. Serve warm.

*According to my kids!

Dips & SAUCES

When I'm in a rush, tired or just couldn't be bothered cooking, there is nothing better than knowing that I just have to put on some pasta and open a jar of homemade sauce and we can have a healthy dinner on the table in less than 10 minutes.

Sauces are brilliant to make ahead, and it really takes no more time to make a quadruple batch than it does to make one. You can store them in sterilised jars or, if you are like me, just freeze them. I portion them into a silicone muffin tray, cover with cling film, freeze and then just pop them into a freezer bag when they are solid. You can also use a mini-muffin tin if you want baby-sized portions. Take them out in the morning to defrost for the evening, or just pop into the microwave and defrost in less than 5 minutes.

EASY-PEASY
BASIL & SPINACH PESTO

MAKES 1 LARGE JAR

A winner with kids and loaded with goodness, you can use this sauce on everything. My favourites are toasted cheese with pesto, pasta with pesto, steak with pesto, chicken with pesto, cherry tomatoes with pesto – or just pesto with pesto. It's that good!

85ml (⅓ cup) extra virgin olive oil

2 large handfuls spinach

1 large handful basil leaves

juice ½ lemon

½ clove garlic, crushed

60g (½ cup) goat's cheese, grated

4 tbsp pumpkin seeds

Place all of the ingredients in a blender, starting with the oil. This helps to break everything up quicker.

Blend until smooth and silky.

Pour into a jar with a lid and refrigerate until you are ready to use. Keeps in the fridge for about 5 days.

HIDDEN VEGGIE
PASTA SAUCE

MAKES ABOUT 500ML (2 CUPS)

The best thing about this sauce is how quickly you can throw it together – that and the fact that it is full of veggies. I always add lots more whole veggies to the dish we're eating this with, so you have loaded sauce and extra whole vegetables. There's no escaping the goodness!

2 tbsp rapeseed oil

1 onion, roughly chopped

2 cloves garlic, crushed

2 red bell peppers, roughly chopped

2 courgettes, sliced

½ head cauliflower, finely chopped

2 large handfuls spinach

4 tbsp tomato purée

800g (29oz) tinned chopped tomatoes

100ml (3½oz) milk of your choice

In a frying pan, heat the rapeseed oil over a low heat. Add the onion and fry for about 10 minutes, until sticky and sweet. Add the garlic and cook for a further minute until fragrant.

Add the peppers, courgettes and cauliflower and cook until the vegetables are al dente – soft but not overcooked.

Sprinkle in the spinach, add the tomato purée and tins of tomatoes, then heat until warmed through.

Pour in the milk and use a stick blender to blend into a smooth sauce.

Cool fully before freezing or storing in jars in the fridge for 3–4 days.

VEGGIE-LOADED
CAULIFLOWER CHEESE SAUCE

MAKES 1 MEDIUM JAR

This sauce is the base for my mac and cheese sauce with a bit of an added twist – it is veggie loaded and super charged. Make ahead and add to pasta as is, serve over cooked vegetables for a yummy side or even pour over potatoes. I guarantee you will all lick your plates clean.

2 tbsp rapeseed oil

1 medium white onion, finely chopped

2 cloves garlic, crushed

60g (¼ cup) butter

2 tbsp flour

250ml (1 cup) milk

1 head cauliflower, roughly chopped and steamed

60g (½ cup) Cheddar cheese

black pepper, to season

1 teaspoon cumin

Heat the oil in a pot over a medium heat. Add the onion and cook until it becomes translucent. Add the garlic and cook for 1–2 minutes more.

Turn the heat to its lowest setting, add the butter, melt, then stir in the flour with a wooden spoon to make a roux.

Cook the flour and butter for about a minute, then slowly whisk in the milk, stirring constantly. The sauce should be silky with no lumps.

Add the cauliflower, cheese, pepper and cumin, then use a stick blender to blend until really smooth.

Use within 2 days in the fridge or freeze.

THE BEST EVER
CURRY-IN-A-HURRY SAUCE

MAKES ABOUT 500ML (2 CUPS)

Add cooked meat or tofu and lots of veggies to this pre-prepared sauce for the ultimate curry in a hurry.

60ml (¼ cup) rapeseed oil

1 large white onion, roughly chopped

6 cloves garlic, crushed

1 large thumb-sized piece root ginger, thinly sliced

2 tsp ground coriander

2 tsp ground cumin

1 tsp turmeric

6 cardamom pods, seeds only

200g (7oz) tinned chopped tomatoes

3 tbsp tomato purée

400ml (14oz) tinned coconut milk

4 tbsp tahini

1 mango, peeled and diced

Heat the rapeseed oil over a medium heat, then gently fry the onion until translucent. Add the garlic and ginger and cook for a further minute or two until fragrant but not browning.

Add all of the spices, chopped tomatoes, tomato purée, coconut milk and tahini, stir well and bring to a simmer.

Pour into a blender with the mango and blend until smooth and creamy.

Pour into sterilised jars and store in the fridge for up to five days or freeze!

5-MINUTE
BLENDER SALSA

MAKES 1 LARGE JAR

Salsa is a great way to get kids eating tomatoes. It's zingy, great for dipping and a cinch to make. Serve with Mexican food or just with crackers and cheese. You can add a little spice to the grown-ups' version by adding a quarter teaspoon of cayenne pepper.

400g (2½ cups) sweet cherry tomatoes
1 sweet onion
juice 1 lime
bunch fresh coriander
½ clove garlic, crushed
black pepper, to season
½ tsp cumin

Place all of the ingredients into a food processor and pulse until you reach your desired consistency. I like it saucy but with small bits of tomatoes still visible.

Store in a sterilised jar in the fridge for up to five days or freeze.

BABY-FRIENDLY
CURRIED HUMMUS

MAKES 1 LARGE JAR

Deliciously fragrant and a winner with kids. This is great for lunches and yummy in a salad sambo too.

4 cloves garlic

400g (15oz) tinned chickpeas, drained

4 tbsp tahini

4 tbsp olive oil, plus extra for drizzling

4 tbsp water

juice 1 lemon

½ tsp grated fresh ginger

1 tsp ground coriander

1 tsp ground cumin

½ tsp ground turmeric

¼ tsp ground cinnamon

6 cardamom pods – deseeded and seeds crushed

¼ tsp ground nutmeg

small bunch fresh coriander, finely chopped

½ tsp cumin seeds (optional)

Preheat the oven to 180°C/350°F/gas 4.

Wrap the garlic cloves in foil and bake for about 20 minutes. It is important to do this for baby hummus, as raw garlic is difficult to digest. When cooked, remove the skins.

Place all of the ingredients, except the coriander and cumin seeds, in a blender and blend until smooth. Add more water, a tablespoon at a time, if it's too thick.

Sprinkle the fresh coriander and cumin seeds on top, lightly drizzle with a little olive oil and serve with soft pitta bread or vegetables. Also makes a great spread for toast.

3-INGREDIENT
PIZZA SAUCE

ENOUGH FOR 8 PIZZA TOASTIES

My go-to pizza sauce, great for proper pizza dough, pizza toasties (see p. 77), tortilla pizzas or even bagel pizzas. I always make it as I need it because it takes less than five minutes, and it's brilliant for when your kids' friends come to play and they want nothing but pizza.

1 tube tomato purée
1 clove garlic, crushed
black pepper, to season
1 tbsp water (I'm not counting this in my 3 ingredients!)

Add all of the ingredients to a bowl and stir really well.

Spread over toasted bread, then top with some veggies and a sprinkle of cheese.

Place under the grill until the cheese melts.

EGG-FREE
AIOLI

MAKES 1 SMALL JAR

Raw eggs should not be given to babies and, personally, I am not a fan either. However, I really like to have a dip for healthy fries, chicken or even a salad wrap. This is my version of an egg-free mayo-type sauce and it is delicious! I make it when I need it and use it fresh, although it keeps in the fridge covered for a few days.

125ml (½ cup) Greek yogurt
1 tbsp apple cider vinegar
1 tsp Dijon mustard
1 tbsp lemon juice
¼ tsp black pepper
1 tsp garlic powder

Add all of the ingredients to a bowl and stir well.

Keep refrigerated (not suitable for freezing).

NOTELLA
EASY-PEASY CHOCOLATE SPREAD

MAKES 1 LARGE JAR

When we go on holidays, one of my kids' favourite things to get is churros with Nutella dip. It is so full of sugar that I had to make up a version of my own. There is a knack to making this spread but it's well worth the effort.

600g (20oz) hazelnuts
2 tbsp coconut oil
2 tbsp cacao powder
4 tbsp maple syrup

Preheat the oven to 180°C/350°F/gas 4.

Place the hazelnuts on a baking tray and put in the oven for 12 minutes, until warmed through and the skins are a darker brown.

Place the nuts into a clean tea towel, then rub together until the skins have come off.

Add the skinless nuts to a food processor and process on full speed. It should take roughly 5–7 minutes for them to turn into a smooth, oily hazelnut butter.

When it's really oily, turn the processor on full again and add the coconut oil and cacao powder. Blend until smooth and chocolatey.

Use a spatula to stir in the maple syrup until fully combined – don't use the processor. (This is important, as the food processor will make the mixture crumbly once the maple syrup is added.)

Pour the spread into a jar and leave in the fridge to set. Keeps in the fridge for a week – if you hide it well from your little ones!

BLACKBERRY, BLACKCURRANT OR STRAWBERRY JAM

MAKES 1 LARGE JAR

600g (2½ cups) blackberries or blackcurrants or strawberries

4 tbsp chia seeds

1 tsp maple syrup to sweeten
(if fruit is not sweet enough)

Wash the fruit in a sieve under a running tap. Shake, then add to a saucepan.

Place over a medium to low heat and gently warm the berries. They will release plenty of liquid.

Turn the heat down to a simmer and allow the berries to cook until soft, then use a fork to mash until really smooth.

Stir in the chia seeds and taste for sweetness. If necessary, add a little amount of maple syrup to sweeten.

Store in a jar in the fridge for up to a week, or freeze in ice-cube trays to use as needed.

Nourishing Snacks &
OCCASIONAL TREATS

The words 'nourishing' and 'treats' don't always go hand in hand, but you definitely won't have trouble getting your little ones to eat these!

Sugary treats should be occasional so I have split this section into:

Nourishing Snacks

Occasional Treats

Nourishing

SNACKS

These are all nutritious, easy to make and perfect for your little ones to eat every day. These are the snacks I keep in the freezer or cupboard for between meals.

HEALTHY
STRAWBERRY BLONDIES

MAKES 16

These delicious blondies are easy to make and kids love them. Making a double batch is just as easy as making one, and they are brilliant for the freezer!

250g (1¼ cups) cashew butter

2 tbsp maple syrup

2 eggs

2 bananas

1 tbsp vanilla extract

1 tsp baking powder

100g (¾ cup) coconut flour

200g (1 cup) fresh strawberries, hulled and cut into quarters

Preheat oven to 180°C/350°F/gas 4.

Mix the cashew butter, maple syrup, eggs, bananas and vanilla until they are lovely and gooey and totally smooth. I use my food processor but you can also use an electric whisk or do it the good old-fashioned way – with a wooden spoon.

Fold in the baking powder and coconut flour and stir until fully combined, then pour the batter into a 26 x 20cm (10 x 8in) tin lined with parchment paper.

Spread the mixture evenly with a spatula, then scatter the strawberries on top. Push them into the cake mixture so that none are sticking out fully.

Bake for 20–25 minutes, until the top is golden.

Allow to cool fully before slicing into 16 squares.

Freeze into pops for smaller babies!

PEANUT BUTTER AND SWEET POTATO CHOCOLATE MOUSSE

SERVES 2 ADULTS & 2 CHILDREN

The combo of sweet potato, peanut butter and chocolate doesn't really sound like much until you put a spoonful into your mouth – you will never look back! You can also make these into ice-pops.

120g (½ cup) peanut butter

300g (1½ cup) cooked sweet potato

4 Medjool dates, soaked in hot water for 10 minutes

400ml (13oz) tinned full-fat coconut milk

3 tbsp cacao powder

1 tsp vanilla extract

To serve

1 banana, chopped

3 tbsp ground peanuts

2 tsp desiccated coconut

sprinkle of cacao powder

Add the peanut butter and sweet potato to a blender.

Drain the Medjool dates and add to the blender with the coconut milk, cacao powder and vanilla extract.

Blend for 5–7 minutes, until the mixture becomes light and airy.

Spoon into small bowls and leave in the fridge to set for about 2 hours. Alternatively, if you want to make ice-pops, pour into moulds and freeze for 4 hours until hard.

To serve the mousse, add some slices of banana, sprinkle over some finely chopped nuts and coconut, then sprinkle over a little extra cacao powder.

AILEEN'S TIP!

For grown-up bowls, you can add chunkier pieces of nuts – just remember to keep them fine for smaller babies and toddlers.

BLUEBERRY & COCONUT
OAT BARS

MAKES 24

In one year, the recipe page for these bars was visited over 300,000 times! I have received so many mails asking why it wasn't in my first book that I had to include it here. They are so easy to make and are perfect to freeze so you always have healthy treats on hand.

180g (1¼ cups) oats
140g (1 cup) buckwheat flour
1 tsp baking powder
40g (¼ cup) desiccated coconut
100g (½ cup) coconut oil
2 bananas, mashed
3 tbsp maple syrup
1 egg
1 tsp vanilla extract
280g (10oz) blueberries
2 tbsp water
1 tbsp chia seeds

Preheat oven to 180°C/350°F/gas 4.

Add the oats, flour, baking powder and 30g of the desiccated coconut to a bowl. Stir, then make a well in the middle and add the coconut oil, bananas, maple syrup, egg and vanilla. Stir until it is fully combined and has formed a dough.

Line a 26 x 20cm (10 x 8in) tin with parchment paper, then pour in three-quarters of the mixture and press it down with a spoon.

Make the blueberry compote by adding the blueberries and water to a saucepan. Bring to the boil then turn the heat down to low and, using a wooden spoon or masher, mash until the blueberries are broken up. Add the chia seeds and stir well.

Pour the blueberry compote over the oat mixture, then dollop the remaining oat mixture on top in small clumps.

Sprinkle over the remaining desiccated coconut, then bake for 15 minutes.

Remove from the oven and cool fully before slicing into 24 small baby bites.

COURGETTE
CHOCOLATE MINI CAKES

MAKES 12

I dare anyone to say they can taste the courgette in these cakes! They are chocolatey, delicious and have so much added goodness that you'll be smiling from ear to ear every time your little ones ask you to make them.

1 medium courgette, grated
225g (1¾ cups) plain flour
1 tsp baking powder
2 tbsp cacao powder
1 banana, mashed
125ml (½ cup) milk
1 egg
2 tbsp rapeseed oil
2 tbsp maple syrup
1 tsp vanilla extract

Preheat the oven to 170°C/340°F/gas 3.

Place the grated courgette into a clean tea towel and squeeze out the liquid. Add the courgette, flour, baking powder and cacao to a bowl. Make a well in the centre and set aside.

In a separate jug, whisk together the remaining ingredients until creamy. Slowly pour the wet mixture into the courgette and flour mix, and whisk until fully combined and silky smooth.

Divide the batter between lightly oiled mini-muffin moulds.

Bake for 15–20 minutes, until brown and a wooden skewer comes out clean.

Cool on a wire rack before serving.

SUPER-HEALTHY
CHICKPEA COOKIES

MAKES 16

When you think of chickpeas you probably think of hummus, but they are an amazing sweet treat too. Topped with toasted, finely crushed nuts, these cookies are filling and healthy for kids of all ages.

400g (15oz) tinned chickpeas, drained

2 large bananas

2 tbsp maple syrup

1 tsp baking powder

130g (½ cup) peanut butter

30g (⅛ cup) butter or coconut oil, melted

1 tsp vanilla

50g (½ cup) oats

4 tbsp finely crushed nuts or seeds, for topping

Preheat oven to 180°C/350°F/gas 4.

Add all of the ingredients, except the nuts or seeds, to a food processor and process until smooth.

Spoon heaped tablespoons of the mixture onto a baking tray lined with parchment paper, and repeat until all of the mixture is gone.

Sprinkle over a little of the topping and bake for 15 minutes, until the cookies are golden.

Cool fully before serving.

CHOCOLATE
TRUFFLE POPS

| MAKES 12 | |

Anything on a stick works like a dream in our house but especially chocolate! Paper straws cut in half work really well for small hands. I made these using a secret veggie that your little ones will never guess is there …

For the truffles
90g (1 cup) oats
135g (½ cup) peanut butter
6 Medjool dates
1 courgette, finely grated, squeezed and drained
1 tbsp coconut oil
60ml (¼ cup) milk of your choice
2 tsp cacao powder

For the chocolate coating
100g (½ cup) cacao butter
1 tbsp maple syrup
1 tsp sugar-free vanilla extract
1 tbsp cacao powder
2 tbsp tahini

Place all of the ingredients for the truffles into a processor, then process until it forms a dough.

Divide the dough into roughly 12 pieces, roll into balls, then stick a paper straw into each one and refrigerate for about 1 hour, until they're cold and hard.

When the truffles are set, bring a saucepan of water, roughly a quarter full, to the boil and then reduce to a simmer. Add the cacao butter to a glass bowl and place over the pan of water to melt, making sure no water gets into the butter and the water doesn't touch the bottom of the bowl.

Remove the bowl from the heat and whisk in the maple syrup, vanilla, cacao powder and tahini until the mixture is completely smooth and creamy. Leave aside to cool and thicken slightly.

Remove the truffles from the fridge, dunk into the chocolate and replace in the fridge until set.

5-MINUTE
CHOCOLATE PEANUT BUTTER NICE CREAM

SERVES 2 ADULTS & 2 CHILDREN

Ice cream is one of our favourite treats, as are chocolate and peanut butter. So when you combine all these it becomes the ultimate treat for mums and dads – I mean, kids!

For the nice cream
4 frozen bananas
125ml (½ cup) milk of your choice
70g (¼ cup) peanut butter
1 tbsp cacao powder
1 tsp vanilla extract

To serve
2 tbsp Notella (see page 232)
4 tbsp finely crushed peanuts

Place all of the ingredients for the nice cream into a blender and pulse until smooth and creamy.

Spoon into serving bowls, then top with a little Notella and a sprinkling of nuts. Just make sure the nuts are finely crushed for babies.

BROWN BREAD
ICE-CREAM CONES

MAKES 4

The video for this recipe has been viewed over 600,000 times, and it is probably the most creative recipe I've ever come up with. Honestly – give them a go!

For the cones

4 slices brown bread
(I get mine in our local bakery, so it's full of good stuff!)

1 tbsp coconut oil, melted

1 tbsp maple syrup

For the nice cream

2 bananas, sliced and frozen

150g (5oz) pineapple, sliced and frozen

125ml (½ cup) coconut milk

Preheat oven to 180°C/350°F/gas 4.

Take a piece of light cardboard and cut it to the size of a dinner plate (I use an old cereal box). Then cut the circle into quarters, twist into cone shapes and wrap with foil to make little tinfoil cones. (You can also use tin cone moulds if you have them.)

Take a slice of bread and, using a rolling pin, roll until really flat. Then lightly brush both sides with coconut oil and one side with maple syrup.

Cut into a large circle about 10cm in diameter. Wrap the bread around the cone mould, maple syrup side facing out, then place on a baking sheet. Repeat with the remaining slices of bread.

Bake for 15 minutes, remove from the oven and leave to cool fully.

Meanwhile, add the frozen bananas, pineapple and coconut milk to a blender and blend until smooth. Pour into a dish, cover with cling film and freeze for 2–4 hours.

Carefully remove the bread from the cone moulds, scoop nice cream into cones and serve.

SUPER HEALTHY
BANANA SPLITS

MAKES 4

Get the little ones involved in making these with you. They will love putting their own together to show you how brilliantly creative they are.

4 bananas

4 tbsp Greek yogurt

4 strawberries, diced

8 raspberries

4 tsp strawberry jam
(see page 234)

4 tsp Notella (see page 232)

2 tbsp desiccated coconut

sprinkle of granola to serve
(see page 34)

Slice each banana lengthways, then place into serving bowls.

Spoon the Greek yogurt into a bowl, stir until really creamy, then add a dollop on top of each banana.

Scatter the strawberries and raspberries over each bowl.

Add a teaspoon of strawberry jam to each portion, then a teaspoon of Notella.

Finally, sprinkle over some desiccated coconut and a little granola to serve.

HEALTHY RAINBOW
SPRINKLES

MAKES 1 MEDIUM JAR

Sprinkles are something that most kids love, but they are full of sugar and artificial colouring. These sprinkles are not only easy to make, but they also last in an airtight jar for months.

For the orange sprinkles
2 tbsp desiccated coconut
¼ tsp turmeric
2 tbsp water

For the pink sprinkles
2 tbsp desiccated coconut
½ tsp beetroot powder, or juice of ½ beetroot
2 tbsp water

For the green sprinkles
2 tbsp desiccated coconut
½ tsp spirulina
2 tbsp water

Preheat oven to 140°C/275°F/gas 1.

Using a separate bowl for each colour, mix all the ingredients together. Stir well, then leave aside for about 15 minutes, until the coconut absorbs the liquid.

Empty each bowl onto a baking tray, making sure the different colours don't touch (this gives the most vibrant colours).

Bake in the oven for 40 minutes, tossing gently halfway through.

Serve over nice cream, cakes, pies, cream, custard, muffins, brownies, fruit, yogurt, smoothies ...
The world needs more sprinkles!

ZINGY
MANGO MOUSSE

SERVES 2 ADULTS & 2 CHILDREN

A scrumptious blend of mango, Greek yogurt and turmeric. Healthy, delicious and a perfect dessert for any day.

1 tbsp grass-fed gelatine

4 tbsp water

1 mango, peeled and roughly chopped

1 lemon, zest and juice

500ml (1¾ cups) Greek yogurt

To serve

4 tbsp Greek yogurt

¼ fresh mango, diced

In a bowl, whisk the gelatine and water, then leave aside until it thickens.

Meanwhile, add the mango and lemon juice to a blender and blend until silky. Pour into a saucepan, place over a medium heat and bring to a bubble.

Add the gelatine mixture to the mango and whisk until smooth. Remove from the heat and allow to cool to about room temperature (don't allow it to set at this point).

Whisk in the Greek yogurt and lemon zest, then pour into serving jars and place in the fridge to set for about an hour.

To serve, top with a little Greek yogurt and diced mango.

FRUIT
STICKS

MAKES 6

A super-easy but very delicious treat for kids and a guaranteed hit. At every party these are the first to disappear.

For the fruit sticks

6 blueberries

6 raspberries

6 strawberries

6 cubes pineapple

2 slices melon, cut into star shapes

For the dipping sauces

100g (½ cup) strawberries

2 tsp ground chia seeds

4 tbsp natural yogurt

4 tbsp Notella (see page 232)

Starting with a blueberry and ending with a melon star, push a piece of each fruit in turn onto an ice-pop stick. Continue until all the fruit has been used. Place the fruit sticks on a serving tray, leaving enough space for three ramekins.

Add the 100g strawberries to a blender and blend until smooth. Stir in the chia seeds then pour into a ramekin.

Spoon the natural yogurt and Notella into separate ramekins.

Serve and let your little ones dip the fruit into the sauces.

RAINBOW
ROCKET POPS

MAKES 6

Veggie pops that will cool your little ones down in no time – full of natural colours and loaded with vitamins and minerals. You will need a little time to let each layer freeze before adding the next, so all that's needed are some rocket-pop moulds and a teeny bit of patience.

For the carrot layer
2 carrots
125ml (½ cup) coconut water
juice ½ lemon

For the beetroot layer
1 beetroot
125ml (½ cup) coconut water
juice ½ lemon

For the spinach layer
2 large handfuls spinach leaves
125ml (½ cup) apple juice
juice ½ lemon

Start with the carrot. Add all of the ingredients to a blender and blend until completely smooth. Divide the mixture between the ice-pop moulds then freeze for about an hour, until they are almost solid.

Repeat with the beetroot mixture – blend then pour into the moulds and freeze for another hour.

Finally, do the same with the spinach mixture.

Freeze until the pops are fully frozen.

AILEEN'S TIP!
I bought great rocket moulds on Amazon, but you can use any ice-pop mould you like!

NUT-FREE
BABY FLAPJACKS

MAKES 24

Packed with seeds and lightly spiced, these flapjacks are great for little ones when you're out and about. You can also crumble them up and sprinkle over Greek yogurt for another yummy treat.

70g (½ cup) pumpkin seeds
80g (½ cup) flaxseeds
70g (½ cup) sesame seeds
180g (2 cups) oats
1 tsp ground cinnamon
½ tsp ground nutmeg
3 bananas
3 tbsp maple syrup
4 tbsp rapeseed or coconut oil
1 tsp vanilla extract

Preheat oven to 150°C/300°F/gas 2.

Use a pestle and mortar to grind the pumpkin seeds until they resemble fine breadcrumbs, then add them to a bowl along with the flaxseeds, sesame seeds, oats, cinnamon and nutmeg.

Place the bananas, maple syrup, oil and vanilla into a blender and blend until smooth and silky, then pour into the oat and seed mixture and stir well.

Pour the mixture into a 26 x 20cm (10 x 8in) baking tin lined with parchment paper. Use a spatula to spread the mixture evenly, then use a large spoon to press it down hard and really compress it.

Bake for 40 minutes, then remove from the oven. Leave to cool fully before slicing into 24 little bars.

Store in an airtight container for up to a week.

OAT-FREE
PEANUT BUTTER BALLS

MAKES 16

These are my favourite and I usually make them then hide them from my kids (only joking – or am I?). They are a great source of protein, really filling and the kids love them more than me. Hide them quick!

140g (1 cup) buckwheat flour

135g (⅔ cup) smooth peanut butter

2 tbsp maple syrup

2 tbsp pea protein powder (optional)

1 tbsp coconut oil

Place all of the ingredients in a food processor and pulse until it forms a dough.

Take tablespoons of the mixture and roll into balls.

Leave in the fridge to set for about an hour before eating.

SUPER-HEALTHY
BLACK BEAN BROWNIES

MAKES 24

Kid-friendly, gooey, sticky chocolate brownies made using black beans. If you love chocolate and you love brownies then these are for you!

For the brownies
400g (15oz) tinned black beans
70g (½ cup) oats
3tbsp cacao powder
1 tsp baking powder
80g (⅓ cup) butter, melted
4 tbsp maple syrup
2 eggs

For the frosting
1 avocado, peeled and stoned
1 tbsp coconut oil
1 tbsp cacao powder
1 tbsp maple syrup

finely ground pistachios or seeds, to decorate

Preheat oven to 180°C/350°F/gas 4.

Add all of the brownie ingredients to a food processor and blend until smooth and fully combined.

Turn into a 26 x 20cm (10 x 8in) tin lined with parchment paper and tap the tin 2–3 times to remove any bubbles.

Bake for 25 minutes, until a skewer comes out clean. Then remove from the oven and leave to cool fully.

Meanwhile, make the frosting by adding all of the frosting ingredients to a clean food processor and blending until silky and creamy.

Spread over the cooled brownies and sprinkle the finely ground pistachios or seeds on top. Slice into squares and serve.

Occasional
TREATS

These are also nutritious but are a
little more indulgent and should be
eaten occasionally – say, on weekends.
Treats taste better when they are
occasional anyway!

BLUEBERRY & APPLE
SMASH CAKE

MAKES A 20CM CAKE

This is one of the most popular recipes on the Baby-Led Feeding website. I've received thousands of photos of the final cakes – and sometimes there's even a little baby munching away too. It's healthy, it looks amazing and it's easy.

2 Pink Lady apples, washed, cored and cut into small chunks

60ml (¼ cup) water

150g (¾ cups) coconut oil, melted and cooled

2 bananas

4 tbsp maple syrup

2 tsp vanilla extract

4 eggs

150g (1¼ cup) buckwheat flour

30g (¼ cup) coconut flour

30g (¼ cup) almond flour or plain flour

3 tsp baking powder

1 tsp cinnamon

½ tsp nutmeg

100g (1 cup) fresh blueberries, plus extra for decorating

For the frosting

200g (1 cup) soft cream cheese

1 lemon, zest, plus juice of ½

2 tbsp maple syrup

Preheat oven to 180°C/350°F/gas 4.

Place the apples in a saucepan with the water. Bring to the boil then simmer for 12 minutes, until soft. Leave aside to cool fully, then add to a blender with the coconut oil, bananas, maple syrup and vanilla and blend until smooth and creamy.

Crack the eggs into a large bowl and using an electric whisk, whisk the eggs until they double in size and become light and airy. To check if they're done, lift the whisk out and swirl a little of the mixture around. If it holds its shape then you've got the right consistency.

Fold in the apple and banana mixture but don't over-mix. This will ensure the cake is light and airy.

In a separate bowl, mix the flours, baking powder and spices, then fold this into the batter.

Finally, add the 100g of blueberries and pour into a lightly oiled cake mould – I use a number 1 mould from Amazon, which measures 30 x 17cm (12 x 6¾in).

Bake for 20 minutes, turn the cake around, then bake for a further 20 minutes to ensure it cooks evenly. Cool fully before frosting.

To make the frosting, beat the cheese, lemon juice, zest and maple syrup with a wooden spoon, then spread over the cake. Decorate with the extra blueberries and serve.

SUPER-YUMMY
BABY DOUGHNUTS

MAKES 12

Be warned! These doughnuts are highly addictive and you will end up making them again and again!

3 bananas
250ml (1 cup) buttermilk
50g (¼ cup) coconut oil, melted
1 tbsp vanilla extract
150g (1¼ cups) buckwheat flour
2 tsp baking powder
½ tsp baking soda

For decorating
1 tbsp coconut oil, melted
1 tbsp coconut sugar
¼ tsp dried cinnamon

Preheat oven to 220°C/425°F/gas 7.

Add the bananas, buttermilk, coconut oil and vanilla to a food processor and process until completely smooth and creamy.

With the processor still running, slowly add the flour, baking powder and baking soda and mix until fully combined.

Pour the batter into a lightly oiled doughnut tin.

Bake for 8–10 minutes, until the tops of the doughnuts are golden, then remove and leave on a wire rack until cool.

To decorate, lightly brush the tops and sides of the doughnuts with the melted coconut oil until covered.

Mix the coconut sugar with the cinnamon, then sprinkle over the doughnuts and eat!

APPLE & CINNAMON FRITTERS

SERVES 2 ADULTS & 2 CHILDREN

Delicious, sweet fritters are an ideal treat for any occasion. I use sweet, crispy apples and serve with a little coconut sugar for the ultimate indulgence.

4 sweet eating apples, peeled, cored and sliced into rings
1 tbsp rapeseed or coconut oil
½ tsp cinnamon

For the batter
130g (1⅛ cup) plain flour
1 tsp baking powder
1 tsp cinnamon
½ tsp nutmeg
185ml (¾ cup) milk
1 egg
1 tsp vanilla extract
2 tbsp melted butter
250ml (1 cup) rapeseed oil, for frying
¼ tsp coconut sugar per portion, to serve

Preheat oven to 180°C/350°F/gas 4.

Place the apple rings on a baking tray lined with parchment paper. Drizzle over the rapeseed oil and cinnamon and use your fingers to completely coat both sides.

Bake in the oven for 10 minutes, until the apple is soft but not floppy, then remove from the oven and cool fully.

To make the batter, add the dry ingredients to a stand mixer.

In a jug, whisk together the milk, egg, vanilla and melted butter, then turn on the mixer and pour the wet mixture into the flour. You can also do this by hand with a whisk.

Heat the rapeseed oil in a frying pan, then dip the apple rings into the batter and fry, about three at a time, until golden on both sides. This should take around 5 minutes.

Remove from the oil and place onto a plate lined with kitchen paper.

Sprinkle with a little coconut sugar to serve.

SUGAR-FREE CHOCOLATE
CHUNKY MINI MUFFINS

MAKES 24

Muffins are a great treat for kids and the best thing about this recipe is that, apart from being delicious, it contains some hidden veggies. Not one person in my family has noticed yet!

140g (1 cup) plain flour

1 tsp baking soda

2 tbsp cacao powder

4 ripe bananas

1 tsp vanilla extract

2 eggs

125ml (½ cup) Greek yogurt (or coconut yogurt for dairy free)

125ml (½ cup) milk of your choice

4 tbsp rapeseed or coconut oil

2 carrots, finely grated

150g (5oz) good quality raw chocolate, cut into chunks

Preheat oven to 170°C/340°F/gas 3.

Add the flour, baking soda and cacao powder to a bowl and stir. Make a well in the centre and leave aside.

In a jug, mash the bananas until smooth, then whisk in the vanilla, eggs, yogurt, milk and oil.

Pour the wet mixture into the flour mixture, stirring well as you do, until fully combined. Then stir in the carrot.

Fold the chocolate chunks into the batter.

Spoon the mixture into a lightly oiled mini-muffin tin, then bake for 20 minutes, until a skewer comes out clean.

Cool on a wire rack before serving.

COCONUT
CHOCOLATE BITES

MAKES 12

Kind of like chocolate macaroons, these delicious bites can be eaten straight from the freezer, so they're a handy treat for busy days.

4 egg whites

1 tbsp maple syrup

1 tbsp cacao powder

2 tbsp macca powder (optional)

240g (2½ cups) desiccated coconut

100g (3½oz) good quality raw chocolate, melted

Preheat oven to 180°C/350°F/gas 4.

Whisk the egg whites with the maple syrup, cacao and macca powder until they form stiff peaks.

Use a spatula to fold in the desiccated coconut – don't over-stir.

Use an ice-cream scoop to divide the mixture onto a baking tray lined with parchment paper.

Bake for 25 minutes, until golden brown, then remove from the oven and cool fully.

When cool, drizzle with the melted chocolate, then refrigerate to set fully before serving.

CHOCOLATE
OATY COOKIES

MAKES 16

Oats are not only wholesome: they are also a slow-release food, so they'll give your very busy little ones lots of energy throughout the day.

100g (1 cup) oats
150g (1¼ cups) buckwheat flour
1 tsp baking powder
1 medium carrot, finely grated
1 medium courgette, finely grated
2 tsp vanilla extract
1 tbsp flaxseeds
3 tbsp maple syrup
120g (½ cup) coconut oil, melted
2 tsp cacao powder
100g (½ cup) smooth peanut butter
100g (3½ oz) good quality raw chocolate

Preheat oven to 180°C/350°F/gas 4.

Add the oats, buckwheat and baking powder to a bowl, and mix well.

In a separate bowl, add the rest of the ingredients except the chocolate and mix until smooth and silky. Pour into the oat mixture and stir until it forms a dough.

Shape the dough into small baby-sized cookies and place on a baking tray lined with parchment paper.

Bake for 15 minutes, until slightly browned. Remove and cool fully before covering with chocolate.

Place the chocolate in a bowl over a saucepan of simmering water until melted, then dip each cookie in, covering just one side.

Refrigerate for about 15 minutes, until the chocolate has fully set.

GINGER
SNAPPING COOKIES

MAKES 24

These cookies are great to make with small kids. They're really quick too, which helps when you have an impatient three-year-old oven-watching.

270g (1⅛ cup) natural peanut butter

1 egg

2 tbsp maple syrup

1 tsp ground ginger

½ tsp ground cinnamon

45g (½ cup) oats

Preheat oven to 180°C/350°F/gas 4.

Place all of the wet ingredients into a large bowl and stir well until fully combined.

Stir in the spices and oats and mix until it comes together as a dough.

Divide the mixture into 24 pieces, roll into balls, then use a fork to flatten slightly.

Bake for 12 minutes, and allow to cool fully before serving.

I REALLY LOVE YOU
JAMMIE DODGERS

MAKES 12

Jammie Dodgers are so popular with kids. These are my healthy version with lots of added benefits. A cookie that is good for you? Yes, please!

130g (1 cup) coconut flour

120g (1 cup) buckwheat flour or plain flour

1 tsp baking powder

140g (½ cup) cashew butter or regular butter

2 eggs

3 tbsp maple syrup

2 tsp vanilla extract

125ml (½ cup) strawberry jam (see page 234)

Preheat oven to 160°C/325°F/gas 3.

Place flours and baking powder in a mixing bowl.

Add the cashew butter, eggs, maple syrup and vanilla to a blender and blend into a purée.

Slowly add the flour mixture until fully combined. If the mixture is too crumbly, add a little water until it comes together.

Wrap in cling film and leave in the fridge to rest for about an hour.

Split the dough into 2 parts to make it easier to roll out. Roll each part to roughly 0.5cm thick and, using a 6cm (2½in) round cutter, cut out 24 cookies. Using a little heart- or star-shaped cutter, cut a heart or star out of the centre of 12 of the cookies.

Place on a baking tray lined with parchment paper and bake for 8–10 minutes or until golden. Watch them carefully so they don't burn. When done, remove and place on a wire rack to cool.

Spoon a heaped teaspoon of jam onto the plain cookies, then place a cookie with a heart or star shape cut out onto each one and press down.

Leave in the fridge for an hour or so, until the jam is set, then enjoy.

PEANUT BUTTER & JELLY
CHOCOLATE CUPS

MAKES 24

Easy to make and perfect for rainy days when you're looking for a fun art project to do with the kids. This one has the added benefit of being able to eat it afterwards!

350g (12oz) good quality raw chocolate

4 tbsp peanut butter

4 tbsp strawberry jam (see page 234)

Place the chocolate in a bowl over a pan of simmering water until it melts.

Line a mini-muffin tin with mini-muffin cases, then half fill each one with some melted chocolate. Place into the fridge and allow to set for about 15 minutes.

Spoon ½ tsp peanut butter, then ½ tsp strawberry jam into each one. Use the spoon to make sure the fillings are not against the edges.

Fill the cases with the remaining melted chocolate to completely cover the peanut butter and jam, then refrigerate for another 15–20 minutes, until fully set.

ANYTIME
RICE SQUARES

MAKES 16

A healthy alternative to Rice Krispie Squares, these are made using only ingredients you will feel good about giving to your kids. Make a triple batch!

4 tbsp maple syrup

2 tbsp coconut oil

1 tsp vanilla extract

140g (⅔ cup) smooth peanut butter

3 tbsp macca powder

2 cups (50 g) natural puffed rice

100g (3½oz) good quality raw chocolate, melted

Add the maple syrup, coconut oil, vanilla and peanut butter to a saucepan and gently heat, stirring well, until smooth and silky.

Whisk in the macca powder until fully combined.

Place the puffed rice in a large bowl, then pour over the warm mixture. Stir well.

Pour into a 20 x 20cm (8 x 8in) baking tin lined with parchment paper, then use a spatula to flatten.

Drizzle with the chocolate, then refrigerate until the mixture is completely set.

Cut into squares and serve.

BABY
BANOFFEE BITES

MAKES 24

There are a few parts to this recipe, so it takes a little time – but, honestly, it is so, so worth it. The only problem is being pestered to make them again!

For the base

2 Medjool dates, soaked in boiling water for 10 minutes

90g (1 cup) oats, ground into oat flour

1 tsp vanilla extract

1 tbsp flaxseed, soaked in 6 tbsp boiling water

4 tbsp rapeseed or olive oil

For the caramel

2 tbsp maple syrup

50g butter

2 tbsp milk

For the topping

2 bananas, sliced

125ml (½ cup) Greek yogurt

4 squares good quality raw chocolate

Preheat oven to 180°C/350°F/gas 4.

Drain the Medjool dates, then add to a food processor with the remaining base ingredients. Process on high until it comes together like a dough.

Line a mini-muffin tin with mini-muffin cases, then spoon a heaped teaspoon of the base mixture into each one. Using your fingers, mould the dough into the shape of the muffin case, bringing it up the sides and leaving a dip in the middle for the filling.

Bake for 12 minutes, then remove from the oven and allow to cool fully before removing from the cases.

To make the caramel, place the maple syrup into a saucepan and bring to the boil. Reduce the heat to a simmer then add the butter and stir well until the butter melts and the sauce reduces and thickens up. Remove from the heat and whisk in the milk until it becomes a thick caramel sauce then allow to cool fully.

Add 1 tsp of caramel to each case and then a slice of banana. Top each bite with 1 tsp of Greek yogurt, then grate some chocolate on top.

APPLE AND CARAMEL
BITES

MAKES 24

The most amazing combination of ingredients ever! If you are an apple lover, then this is the recipe for you. I usually make a double batch because they don't last long.

180g (2 cups) oats
140g (1 cup) buckwheat flour
1 tsp baking powder
40g (⅓ cup) desiccated coconut
50g (¼ cup) coconut oil, melted
60ml (¼ cup) rapeseed oil
2 bananas, mashed
1 egg
1 tsp vanilla extract
4 sweet eating apples, peeled and diced

For the caramel sauce
2 tbsp maple syrup
50g butter
2 tbsp milk

6 crushed pecan nuts, to decorate

Preheat oven to 180°C/350°F/gas 4.

Place the oats, flour, baking powder and 30g of the desiccated coconut in a bowl. Give everything a good stir, then make a well in the middle and add the coconut oil, bananas, egg and vanilla. Stir well until fully combined and a dough has formed.

Line a 26 x 20cm (10 x 8in) tin with parchment paper, then pour in the mixture and press it down with a spoon.

Scatter the apple over the oat mixture and leave aside.

To make the caramel, place the maple syrup into a saucepan and bring to the boil. Reduce the heat to a simmer then add the butter and stir well until the butter melts and the sauce reduces and thickens up. Remove from the heat and whisk in the milk until it becomes a thick caramel sauce, then pour over the apples.

Sprinkle the pecans and remaining desiccated coconut on top, then bake for 25 minutes.

Allow to cool fully, then slice into portions and serve.

Weekly
MEAL PLANNER

	MONDAY	TUESDAY	WEDNESDAY
BREAKFAST			
LUNCH			
SNACK			
DINNER			

A little planning makes eating healthy every week so much easier. We like to write out our meals for the week and stick it on the fridge. It makes life so much easier for everyone.

THURSDAY	FRIDAY	SATURDAY	SUNDAY

Weekly
MEAL PLANNER

	MONDAY	TUESDAY	WEDNESDAY
BREAKFAST			
LUNCH			
SNACK			
DINNER			

A little planning makes eating healthy every week so much easier. We like to write out our meals for the week and stick it on the fridge. It makes life so much easier for everyone.

THURSDAY	FRIDAY	SATURDAY	SUNDAY

Leabharlann
Contae na Mídhe

INDEX

3-Ingredient Pizza Sauce 230
5-Minute Blender Salsa 226
5-Minute Chocolate Peanut Butter Nice Cream 251
10-Minute Chickpea Burgers 130
15-Minute Tex-Mex Wraps 126

A

aioli, Egg-Free Aioli 231
allergies 15
almond flour, Blueberry and Apple Smash Cake 269
almonds
    Chicken (or Tofu) Tikka Masala 161
    Sweet Orange Carrots 199
Animal Toasties 72–3
Anytime Rice Squares 287
apple juice, Rainbow Rocket Pops 261
apples
    Apple and Caramel Bites 201
    Apple and Cinnamon Fritters 274
    Apple Crumble Parfait 41
    Apple Pie Overnight Oats 30
    Blueberry and Apple Smash Cake 269
    Carrot and Apple Salad 202
    Mammy's Yummy Porridge with Apple, Berries and
        Seeds 48
    Raspberry Porridge Mini Muffins 36
Asian-Spiced Baby Spuds 186
asparagus, One-Pan Lemon and Garlic Chicken with
        Asparagus and Baby Potatoes 147
aubergines, Hummus, Roasted Veggies, Pittas and
        Yogurt Dip 174
avocados
    Chicken and Cheese Quesadillas 81
    Chilli con Veggie with the Trimmings 156
    Fajitas with Pulled Beef and Veggies 175
    Quinoa Falafels in a Bowl of Yum! 150
    Smashed Avo Eggy Toasties 51
    Super-Healthy Black Bean Brownies 267

B

Baby Banoffee Bites 290
Baby Leaves with Fruit Salad 203
Baby-Friendly Curried Hummus 229
Baby-Friendly Irish Chowder 145
Baby-Friendly Veggie Fritters 87
baby-led feeding 14–19
    safety tips 16–17

Baked Bell Peppers with Eggs 57
Baked Pesto Haddock with Garlic Spuds 125
Baked Veggie-Loaded Baby Potatoes 189
bananas 22
    5-Minute Chocolate Peanut Butter Nice Cream 251
    Animal Toasties 72–3
    Apple and Caramel Bites 201
    Apple Crumble Parfait 41
    Apple Pie Overnight Oats 30
    Baby Banoffee Bites 290
    Blueberry and Apple Smash Cake 269
    Blueberry and Coconut Oat Bars 242
    Brown Bread Ice-Cream Cones 253
    Chocolate and Banana Pancakes 62
    Chocolate Spread and Banana Overnight Oats 31
    Courgette Chocolate Mini Cakes 245
    Easy-Peasy Rhubarb Oat Bake 33
    Healthy Strawberry Blondies 239
    Mammy's Yummy Porridge with Peanut Butter,
        Banana and Nutty Sprinkles 49
    Nut and Sugar-Free Fruit Granola 34
    Nut-Free Baby Flapjacks 262
    Oat Pancakes with Blueberries 102
    Oatmeal Power Cookies 27
    Overnight Carrot-Cake Oats 105
    Peanut Butter and Sweet Potato Chocolate Mousse
        241
    Quinoa Pancakes 67
    Sugar-Free Chocolate Chunky Mini Muffins 277
    Super-Healthy Banana Splits 255
    Super-Healthy Chickpea Cookies 247
    Super-Yummy Baby Doughnuts 272
    Toddler-and-Kid-Approved Banana and Walnut
        Muffins 98
    Waffles and Chocolate Nice Cream 68
bars
    Bean and Nut Breakfast Bars 39
    Blueberry and Coconut Oat Bars 242
    Nut-Free Baby Flapjacks 262
Bean and Nut Breakfast Bars 39
Bean and Veggie Bake Bites 215
Bean and Veggie Salad 205
beans
    Beans, Beans, Good for the Heart Salad 90
    Super-Handy Pies 106
    see also black beans; butter beans; green beans; red
        kidney beans

beef
    Fajitas with Pulled Beef and Veggies 175
    Ramen with Sticky Chicken, Beef or Tofu 163
    Stuffed Peppers with Sweet Potato Fries 171
beetroot
    Baby Leaves with Fruit Salad 203
    Chicken Tenders with Roasted Veggies 151
    Fruit and Veggie Salad with Greek Yogurt and
        Granola 94
    Healthy Rainbow Sprinkles 257
    Loveliest Bulgur Wheat Salad 209
    Mammy's Yummy Porridge with Summer Fruits 48
    Rainbow Rocket Pops 261
Best Ever Curry-in-a-Hurry Sauce 225
black beans
    15-Minute Tex-Mex Wraps 126
    Bean and Nut Breakfast Bars 39
    Bean and Veggie Bake Bites 215
    Bean and Veggie Salad 205
    Beans, Beans, Good for the Heart Salad 90
    Chicken and Cheese Quesadillas 81
    Patatas Bravas with Chicken/Beans 118
    Refried Mexican Black Beans 213
    Stuffed Peppers with Sweet Potato Fries 171
    Super-Healthy Black Bean Brownies 267
blackberries
    Blackberry Jam 234–5
    Chocolate and Banana Pancakes 62
Blackcurrant Jam 234–5
blueberries
    Animal Toasties 72–3
    Blueberry and Apple Smash Cake 269
    Blueberry and Coconut Oat Bars 242
    Fruit Sticks 260
    Mammy's Yummy Porridge with Peanut Butter,
        Banana and Nutty Sprinkles 49
    Mammy's Yummy Porridge with Summer Fruits 48
    Oat Pancakes with Blueberries 102
    Quinoa Pancakes 67
    Veggie Toasties with Fruit Salad 52
    Xs and Os Waffles with Raspberries and Blueberries
        71
bread/breadcrumbs
    Animal Toasties 72–3
    Brown Bread Ice-Cream Cones 253
    Brown Bread Roll-Ups 109
    Hidden Veggie Mac and Cheese 177
    Homemade Fish Goujons with Mushy Peas and
        Oven Chips 172
    PBJ Sambo Roll-Ups 111
    Pizza Toasties 77
    Pot o' Mussels with Bread for Dipping 136
    Sweet Potato Grow-Quettes 193
    Thai Fishcakes with Potato Squares 122

Turkey Burgers and Sweet Potato Fries 178
    World's Best Stuffing Balls 216
Breakfast Frittata Mini Muffins 43
broccoli
    Baked Veggie-Loaded Baby Potatoes 189
    Chicken and Broccoli Pot Pies 166
    Coconut Poached Salmon with Miso Veggies and
        Rice 133
    Granny's Fish and Broccoli Pie 154
    Risotto with Goat's Cheese and Peas 208
    Roasted Broccoli 198
    Sweet Potato Grow-Quettes 193
    Sweet and Sour Chickpea and Noodle Stir-Fry 127
    Veggie Toasties with Fruit Salad 52
Brown Bread Ice-Cream Cones 253
Brown Bread Roll-Ups 109
bulgur wheat, Loveliest Bulgur Wheat Salad 209
butter beans
    Bean and Veggie Bake Bites 215
    Bean and Veggie Salad 205
    Beans, Beans, Good for the Heart Salad 90
butternut squash
    Hidden Veggie Mac and Cheese 177
    Loveliest Bulgur Wheat Salad 209
    Super-Handy Pies 106

C

cakes
    Anytime Rice Squares 287
    Apple and Caramel Bites 201
    Baby Banoffee Bites 290
    Blueberry and Apple Smash Cake 269
    Coconut Chocolate Bites 278
    Super-Healthy Black Bean Brownies 267
    Super-Yummy Baby Doughnuts 272
    see also bars; cookies; muffins
carrots
    Baby Leaves with Fruit Salad 203
    Baby-Friendly Irish Chowder 145
    Baby-Friendly Veggie Fritters 87
    Carrot and Apple Salad 202
    Chicken and Broccoli Pot Pies 166
    Chicken Tenders with Roasted Veggies 151
    Chocolate Oaty Cookies 279
    Fruit and Veggie Salad with Greek Yogurt and
        Granola 94
    Hidden Veggie Mac and Cheese 177
    Loveliest Bulgur Wheat Salad 209
    Oatmeal Power Cookies 27
    Overnight Carrot-Cake Oats 105
    Rainbow Rocket Pops 261
    Ramen with Sticky Chicken, Beef or Tofu 163
    Sugar-Free Chocolate Chunky Mini Muffins 277
    Sweet Orange Carrots 199

Index

Sweet Potato and Carrot Curried Hummus with
   10-Minute Falafels 78
Sweet Potato and Carrot Superhero Muffins 95
Sweet Potato Grow-Quettes 193
Veggie-Loaded Mini Muffins 96
cashew butter
   Healthy Strawberry Blondies 239
   Jammie Dodgers 283
cauliflower
   Baby-Friendly Veggie Fritters 87
   Baked Veggie-Loaded Baby Potatoes 189
   Healthy Cauliflower Gratin 206
   Hidden Veggie Mac and Cheese 177
   Hidden Veggie Pasta Sauce 222
   Roasted Cauliflower with Goat's Cheese 196
   Sweet Potato and Cauliflower Cakes 86
   Veggie-Loaded Cauliflower Cheese Sauce 223
   Veggie-Loaded Mini Muffins 96
Cheddar cheese
   15-Minute Tex-Mex Wraps 126
   Baked Bell Peppers with Eggs 57
   Baked Veggie-Loaded Baby Potatoes 189
   Breakfast Frittata Mini Muffins 43
   Chicken and Cheese Quesadillas 81
   Chilli con Veggie with the Trimmings 156
   Fajitas with Pulled Beef and Veggies 175
   Healthy Cauliflower Gratin 206
   Hidden Veggie Mac and Cheese 177
   Macmammy Egg Muffins 54
   Pizza Toasties 77
   Sweet Potato Grow-Quettes 193
   Veggie-Loaded Cauliflower Cheese Sauce 223
   Veggie-Loaded Mini Muffins 96
cheese
   Cottage Cheese Pancakes 63
   Quinoa Falafels in a Bowl of Yum! 150
   Salmon and Prawn Linguine 121
   see also Cheddar cheese; cream cheese; goat's cheese;
      mozzarella; Parmesan cheese
cherry tomatoes
   5-Minute Blender Salsa 226
   10-Minute Chickpea Burgers 130
   15-Minute Tex-Mex Wraps 126
   Baby Leaves with Fruit Salad 203
   Baked Bell Peppers with Eggs 57
   Brown Bread Roll-Ups 109
   Chilli con Veggie with the Trimmings 156
   Kid-Approved Pasta Salad 92
   Loaded Baby Omelette 55
   Moroccan Turkey Meatballs 141
   Pesto Pasta with Grilled Veggies and Balsamic
      Tomatoes 117
   Really Quick Rainbow Pizzas 131
   Salmon and Prawn Linguine 121

Sticky Chicken Tray Bake 142
Turkey Burgers and Sweet Potato Fries 178
Veggie-Loaded Bolognese 152
Veggie-Loaded Mini Quiches 79
chia seeds
   Blackberry, Blackcurrant or Strawberry Jam 234–5
   Blueberry and Coconut Oat Bars 242
   Easy-Peasy Rhubarb Oat Bake 33
   Fruit Sticks 260
   Kid-Happy Chia Pudding 38
chicken
   Chicken and Broccoli Pot Pies 166
   Chicken and Cheese Quesadillas 81
   Chicken (or Tofu) Tikka Masala 161
   Chicken on a Stick with Peanut Sauce 85
   Chicken Tenders with Roasted Veggies 151
   One-Pan Lemon and Garlic Chicken with Asparagus
      and Baby Potatoes 147
   Patatas Bravas with Chicken/Beans 118
   Ramen with Sticky Chicken, Beef or Tofu 163
   Sticky Chicken Tray Bake 142
   Yummy Butter Chicken (or Tofu) 162
chickpeas
   10-Minute Chickpea Burgers 130
   Baby-Friendly Curried Hummus 229
   Hummus, Roasted Veggies, Pittas and Yogurt Dip
      174
   Moroccan Turkey Meatballs 141
   Quinoa Falafels in a Bowl of Yum! 150
   Super-Healthy Chickpea Cookies 247
   Sweet Potato and Carrot Curried Hummus with
      10-Minute Falafels 78
   Sweet and Sour Chickpea and Noodle Stir-Fry 127
Chilli con Veggie with the Trimmings 156
chocolate/cacao powder
   5-Minute Chocolate Peanut Butter Nice Cream 251
   Anytime Rice Squares 287
   Baby Banoffee Bites 290
   Bean and Nut Breakfast Bars 39
   Chocolate and Banana Pancakes 62
   Chocolate Oaty Cookies 279
   Chocolate Spread and Banana Overnight Oats 31
   Chocolate Truffle Pops 248
   Coconut Chocolate Bites 278
   Courgette Chocolate Mini Cakes 245
   Notella Easy-Peasy Chocolate Spread 232
   Oatmeal Power Cookies 27
   Peanut Butter and Jelly Chocolate Cups 285
   Peanut Butter and Sweet Potato Chocolate Mousse
      241
   Sugar-Free Chocolate Chunky Mini Muffins 277
   Super-Healthy Black Bean Brownies 267
   Sweet Potato Orange Pancakes 64
   Waffles and Chocolate Nice Cream 68

clementines
    Fruit and Veggie Salad with Greek Yogurt and
        Granola 94
    Veggie Toasties with Fruit Salad 52
coconut, desiccated
    Apple and Caramel Bites 201
    Blueberry and Coconut Oat Bars 242
    Chicken (or Tofu) Tikka Masala 161
    Coconut Chocolate Bites 278
    Easy-Peasy Rhubarb Oat Bake 33
    Healthy Rainbow Sprinkles 257
    Kid-Happy Chia Pudding 38
    Nut and Sugar-Free Fruit Granola 34
    Peanut Butter and Sweet Potato Chocolate Mousse
        241
    Super-Healthy Banana Splits 255
coconut flour
    Blueberry and Apple Smash Cake 269
    Healthy Strawberry Blondies 239
    Jammie Dodgers 283
coconut milk
    Best Ever Curry-in-a-Hurry Sauce 225
    Brown Bread Ice-Cream Cones 253
    Coconut Poached Salmon with Miso Veggies and
        Rice 133
    Peanut Butter and Sweet Potato Chocolate Mousse
        241
    Yummy Butter Chicken (or Tofu) 162
coconut oil
    Anytime Rice Squares 287
    Apple and Caramel Bites 201
    Apple and Cinnamon Fritters 274
    Blueberry and Apple Smash Cake 269
    Blueberry and Coconut Oat Bars 242
    Brown Bread Ice-Cream Cones 253
    Chocolate Oaty Cookies 279
    Chocolate Truffle Pops 248
    Notella Easy-Peasy Chocolate Spread 232
    Nut-Free Baby Flapjacks 262
    Oat-Free Peanut Butter Balls 264
    Sugar-Free Chocolate Chunky Mini Muffins 277
    Super-Healthy Black Bean Brownies 267
    Super-Healthy Chickpea Cookies 247
    Super-Yummy Baby Doughnuts 272
coconut sugar
    Apple and Cinnamon Fritters 274
    Super-Yummy Baby Doughnuts 272
coconut water, Rainbow Rocket Pops 261
Coeliac Ireland 15
cookies
    Chocolate Oaty Cookies 279
    Ginger Snapping Cookies 280
    Jammie Dodgers 283

    Oatmeal Power Cookies 27
    Super-Healthy Chickpea Cookies 247
Cottage Cheese Pancakes 63
courgettes
    15-Minute Tex-Mex Wraps 126
    Bean and Veggie Bake Bites 215
    Chicken on a Stick with Peanut Sauce 85
    Chilli con Veggie with the Trimmings 156
    Chocolate Oaty Cookies 279
    Chocolate Truffle Pops 248
    Courgette Chocolate Mini Cakes 245
    Fajitas with Pulled Beef and Veggies 175
    Hidden Veggie Pasta Sauce 222
    Hummus, Roasted Veggies, Pittas and Yogurt Dip
        174
    Italian Quinoa Bites 82
    Pesto Pasta with Grilled Veggies and Balsamic
        Tomatoes 117
    Quinoa Falafels in a Bowl of Yum! 150
    Super-Handy Pies 106
    Sweet and Sour Chickpea and Noodle Stir-Fry 127
    Veggie-Loaded Bolognese 152
    Veggie-Loaded Mini Muffins 96
    Veggie-Loaded Mini Quiches 79
crackers
    10-Minute Chickpea Burgers 130
    Chicken Tenders with Roasted Veggies 151
cream cheese
    Animal Toasties 72–3
    Blueberry and Apple Smash Cake 269
cream (sour)
    15-Minute Tex-Mex Wraps 126
    Chilli con Veggie with the Trimmings 156
    Fajitas with Pulled Beef and Veggies 175
    Sweet Potato Fries with 2-Minute Garlic Dip 194
cucumbers
    Brown Bread Roll-Ups 109
    Hummus, Roasted Veggies, Pittas and Yogurt Dip
        174

D
dates 19
    Apple Crumble Parfait 41
    Baby Banoffee Bites 290
    Chocolate Truffle Pops 248
    Peanut Butter and Sweet Potato Chocolate Mousse
        241
dips/sauces 220–31
dragon fruit, Mammy's Yummy Porridge with Summer
        Fruits 48

Index

E

Easy-Peasy Basil and Spinach Pesto 220
Easy-Peasy Rhubarb Oat Bake 33
Egg-Free Aioli 231
eggs
    10-Minute Chickpea Burgers 130
    Apple and Caramel Bites 201
    Apple and Cinnamon Fritters 274
    Baby-Friendly Veggie Fritters 87
    Baked Bell Peppers with Eggs 57
    Bean and Nut Breakfast Bars 39
    Bean and Veggie Bake Bites 215
    Blueberry and Apple Smash Cake 269
    Blueberry and Coconut Oat Bars 242
    Breakfast Frittata Mini Muffins 43
    Chicken and Broccoli Pot Pies 166
    Chicken Tenders with Roasted Veggies 151
    Coconut Chocolate Bites 278
    Cottage Cheese Pancakes 63
    Courgette Chocolate Mini Cakes 245
    Ginger Snapping Cookies 280
    Healthier Pasta Carbonara 128
    Healthy Strawberry Blondies 239
    Homemade Fish Goujons with Mushy Peas and
        Oven Chips 172
    Italian Quinoa Bites 82
    Jammie Dodgers 283
    Loaded Baby Omelette 55
    Loaded Spanish Omelette with Salad 137
    Macmammy Egg Muffins 54
    Oat Pancakes with Blueberries 102
    Oatmeal Power Cookies 27
    Potato and Egg Nests 59
    Potato Rosti 185
    Quinoa Pancakes 67
    Raspberry Porridge Mini Muffins 36
    Smashed Avo Eggy Toasties 51
    Spinach Gnocchi with Pesto and Veggies 168
    Sugar-Free Chocolate Chunky Mini Muffins 277
    Super-Healthy Black Bean Brownies 267
    Sweet Potato and Carrot Superhero Muffins 95
    Sweet Potato and Cauliflower Cakes 86
    Sweet Potato Grow-Quettes 193
    Thai Fishcakes with Potato Squares 122
    Toddler-and-Kid-Approved Banana and Walnut
        Muffins 98
    Turkey Burgers and Sweet Potato Fries 178
    Veggie Toasties with Fruit Salad 52
    Veggie-Loaded Mini Muffins 96
    Veggie-Loaded Mini Quiches 79
    Waffles and Chocolate Nice Cream 68
    Xs and Os Waffles with Raspberries and Blueberries
        71

F

Fajitas with Pulled Beef and Veggies 175
falafels, Sweet Potato and Carrot Curried Hummus
        with 10-Minute Falafels 78
fish
    Baby-Friendly Irish Chowder 145
    Baked Pesto Haddock with Garlic Spuds 125
    Granny's Fish and Broccoli Pie 154
    see also hake; mussels; prawns; salmon
flaxseeds/linseeds
    Apple Pie Overnight Oats 30
    Baby Banoffee Bites 290
    Chocolate Oaty Cookies 279
    Mammy's Yummy Porridge 48–9
    Nut and Sugar-Free Fruit Granola 34
    Nut-Free Baby Flapjacks 262
    Oatmeal Power Cookies 27
frozen food 21–2
Fruit Sticks 260
Fruit and Veggie Salad with Greek Yogurt and Granola
        94

G

Ginger Snapping Cookies 280
gluten 15
gnocchi, Spinach Gnocchi with Pesto and Veggies 168
goat's cheese
    Baby Leaves with Fruit Salad 203
    Easy-Peasy Basil and Spinach Pesto 220
    Loaded Baby Omelette 55
    Risotto with Goat's Cheese and Peas 208
    Roasted Cauliflower with Goat's Cheese 196
    Salmon and Prawn Linguine 121
    Veggie Pizza Scrolls 101
    Granny's Fish and Broccoli Pie 154
granola
    Fruit and Veggie Salad with Greek Yogurt and
        Granola 94
    Nut and Sugar-Free Fruit Granola 34
    Super-Healthy Banana Splits 255
grapes, Baby Leaves with Fruit Salad 203
Greek yogurt
    10-Minute Chickpea Burgers 130
    Apple Crumble Parfait 41
    Baby Banoffee Bites 290
    Chicken (or Tofu) Tikka Masala 161
    Chocolate and Banana Pancakes 62
    Egg-Free Aioli 231
    Fruit and Veggie Salad with Greek Yogurt and
        Granola 94
    Granny's Fish and Broccoli Pie 154
    Healthier Pasta Carbonara 128
    Hummus, Roasted Veggies, Pittas and Yogurt Dip
        174
    Kid-Happy Chia Pudding 38

Loaded Spanish Omelette with Salad 137
Mammy's Yummy Porridge with Apple, Berries and
    Seeds 48
Overnight Carrot-Cake Oats 105
Patatas Bravas with Chicken/Beans 118
Pot o' Mussels with Bread for Dipping 136
Quinoa Falafels in a Bowl of Yum! 150
Raspberry Porridge Mini Muffins 36
Smashed Garlic and Lime Spud Salad 190
Sugar-Free Chocolate Chunky Mini Muffins 277
Super-Healthy Banana Splits 255
Sweet Potato Orange Pancakes 64
Thai Fishcakes with Potato Squares 122
Xs and Os Waffles with Raspberries and Blueberries
    71
Zingy Mango Mousse 258
see also yogurt
green beans
    Baked Pesto Haddock with Garlic Spuds 125
    Spinach Gnocchi with Pesto and Veggies 168
    Thai Fishcakes with Potato Squares 122

H
hake
    Homemade Fish Goujons with Mushy Peas and
        Oven Chips 172
    Thai Fishcakes with Potato Squares 122
hazelnuts
    Chocolate Spread and Banana Overnight Oats 31
    Notella Easy-Peasy Chocolate Spread 232
    World's Best Stuffing Balls 216
Healthier Pasta Carbonara 128
Healthy Cauliflower Gratin 206
Healthy Rainbow Sprinkles 257
Healthy Strawberry Blondies 239
Here Fishy-Fishy Lime, Coriander and Ginger Salmon
    Pops 164
Hidden Veggie Mac and Cheese 177
Hidden Veggie Pasta Sauce 222
Home Fries 188
Homemade Fish Goujons with Mushy Peas and Oven
    Chips 172
hummus
    Baby-Friendly Curried Hummus 229
    Brown Bread Roll-Ups 109
    Hummus, Roasted Veggies, Pittas and Yogurt Dip
        174
    Quinoa Falafels in a Bowl of Yum! 150
    Sweet Potato and Carrot Curried Hummus with
        10-Minute Falafels 78

I
ice-pops 241, 261
iron, sources of 9–10
Italian Quinoa Bites 82

J
jam
    Blackberry, Blackcurrant or Strawberry Jam 234–5
    Jammie Dodgers 283
    Mammy's Yummy Porridge with Apple, Berries and
        Seeds 48
    PBJ Sambo Roll-Ups 111
    Peanut Butter and Jam Overnight Oats 31
    Peanut Butter and Jelly Chocolate Cups 285
    Super-Healthy Banana Splits 255
    Xs and Os Waffles with Raspberries and Blueberries
        71

K
Kid-Approved Pasta Salad 92
Kid-Happy Chia Pudding 38
kiwis
    Fruit and Veggie Salad with Greek Yogurt and
        Granola 94
    Mammy's Yummy Porridge with Summer Fruits 48
    Veggie Toasties with Fruit Salad 52

L
lemons
    10-Minute Chickpea Burgers 130
    Baby-Friendly Curried Hummus 229
    Blueberry and Apple Smash Cake 269
    Carrot and Apple Salad 202
    Easy-Peasy Basil and Spinach Pesto 220
    Egg-Free Aioli 231
    Homemade Fish Goujons with Mushy Peas and
        Oven Chips 172
    Hummus, Roasted Veggies, Pittas and Yogurt Dip
        174
    Kid-Happy Chia Pudding 38
    Loveliest Bulgur Wheat Salad 209
    Mammy's Mushy Peas 200
    Mango and Lime Quinoa 210
    Moroccan Turkey Meatballs 141
    One-Pan Lemon and Garlic Chicken with Asparagus
        and Baby Potatoes 147
    Patatas Bravas with Chicken/Beans 118
    Quinoa Falafels in a Bowl of Yum! 150
    Rainbow Rocket Pops 261
    Raspberry Porridge Mini Muffins 36
    Roasted Broccoli 198
    Stuffed Peppers with Sweet Potato Fries 171
    Sweet Potato and Carrot Curried Hummus with
        10-Minute Falafels 78

Toddler-and-Kid-Approved Banana and Walnut Muffins 98
Veggie-Loaded Bolognese 152
Yummy Butter Chicken (or Tofu) 162
Zingy Mango Mousse 258
lettuce
10-Minute Chickpea Burgers 130
Turkey Burgers and Sweet Potato Fries 178
limes
5-Minute Blender Salsa 226
10-Minute Chickpea Burgers 130
15-Minute Tex-Mex Wraps 126
Baby Leaves with Fruit Salad 203
Bean and Veggie Salad 205
Chicken on a Stick with Peanut Sauce 85
Chilli con Veggie with the Trimmings 156
Coconut Poached Salmon with Miso Veggies and Rice 133
Fajitas with Pulled Beef and Veggies 175
Fruit and Veggie Salad with Greek Yogurt and Granola 94
Here Fishy-Fishy Lime, Coriander and Ginger Salmon Pops 164
Ramen with Sticky Chicken, Beef or Tofu 163
Refried Mexican Black Beans 213
Smashed Garlic and Lime Spud Salad 190
Sweet Potato Fries with 2-Minute Garlic Dip 194
Sweet and Sour Chickpea and Noodle Stir-Fry 127
Thai Fishcakes with Potato Squares 122
Loaded Baby Omelette 55
Loaded Spanish Omelette with Salad 137
Loveliest Bulgur Wheat Salad 209
lunchbox planner 112–13
lunchboxes 22, 77–111

M
Macmammy Egg Muffins 54
Mammy's Mushy Peas 200
Mammy's Yummy Porridge
with Apple, Berries and Seeds 48
with Peanut Butter, Banana and Nutty Sprinkles 49
with Summer Fruits 48
mange tout, Coconut Poached Salmon with Miso Veggies and Rice 133
mangos
Asian-Spiced Baby Spuds 186
Bean and Veggie Salad 205
Best Ever Curry-in-a-Hurry Sauce 225
Fruit and Veggie Salad with Greek Yogurt and Granola 94
Mammy's Yummy Porridge with Summer Fruits 48
Mango and Lime Quinoa 210
Veggie Toasties with Fruit Salad 52
Zingy Mango Mousse 258

maple syrup 19
Anytime Rice Squares 287
Apple Pie Overnight Oats 30
Baby Banoffee Bites 290
Bean and Nut Breakfast Bars 39
Bean and Veggie Salad 205
Beans, Beans, Good for the Heart Salad 90
Blackberry, Blackcurrant or Strawberry Jam 234–5
Blueberry and Apple Smash Cake 269
Blueberry and Coconut Oat Bars 242
Brown Bread Ice-Cream Cones 253
Chocolate Oaty Cookies 279
Chocolate Truffle Pops 248
Courgette Chocolate Mini Cakes 245
Easy-Peasy Rhubarb Oat Bake 33
Ginger Snapping Cookies 280
Healthy Strawberry Blondies 239
Jammie Dodgers 283
Loveliest Bulgur Wheat Salad 209
Notella Easy-Peasy Chocolate Spread 232
Nut-Free Baby Flapjacks 262
Oat-Free Peanut Butter Balls 264
Oatmeal Power Cookies 27
Peanut Butter and Jam Overnight Oats 31
Ramen with Sticky Chicken, Beef or Tofu 163
Sticky Chicken Tray Bake 142
Super-Healthy Black Bean Brownies 267
Super-Healthy Chickpea Cookies 247
Sweet Orange Carrots 199
Sweet and Sour Chickpea and Noodle Stir-Fry 127
melons, Fruit Sticks 260
Moroccan Turkey Meatballs 141
mozzarella
Kid-Approved Pasta Salad 92
Pizza Toasties 77
Really Quick Rainbow Pizzas 131
Stuffed Peppers with Sweet Potato Fries 171
muffins
Macmammy Egg Muffins 54
Raspberry Porridge Mini Muffins 36
Sugar-Free Chocolate Chunky Mini Muffins 277
Sweet Potato and Carrot Superhero Muffins 95
Toddler-and-Kid-Approved Banana and Walnut Muffins 98
Veggie-Loaded Mini Muffins 96
mushrooms, Chicken and Broccoli Pot Pies 166
mussels
Baby-Friendly Irish Chowder 145
Pot o' Mussels with Bread for Dipping 136

N
noodles
Ramen with Sticky Chicken, Beef or Tofu 163
Sweet and Sour Chickpea and Noodle Stir-Fry 127

Notella 232
    Animal Toasties 73
    Chocolate Spread and Banana Overnight Oats 31
    Cottage Cheese Pancakes 63
    Fruit Sticks 260
    Mammy's Yummy Porridge with Peanut Butter,
        Banana and Nutty Sprinkles 49
    Notella Easy-Peasy Chocolate Spread 232
    Super-Healthy Banana Splits 255
Nut and Sugar-Free Fruit Granola 34
Nut-Free Baby Flapjacks 262
nuts
    5-Minute Chocolate Peanut Butter Nice Cream 251
    Mammy's Yummy Porridge with Peanut Butter,
        Banana and Nutty Sprinkles 49
    Super-Healthy Black Bean Brownies 267
    Super-Healthy Chickpea Cookies 247
    Toddler-and-Kid-Approved Banana and Walnut
        Muffins 98
    see also almonds; cashew butter; hazelnuts; peanut
        butter; pecan nuts; pine nuts

O

Oat-Free Peanut Butter Balls 264
oats
    Apple and Caramel Bites 201
    Apple Crumble Parfait 41
    Apple Pie Overnight Oats 30
    Baby Banoffee Bites 290
    Bean and Nut Breakfast Bars 39
    Blueberry and Coconut Oat Bars 242
    Chocolate Oaty Cookies 279
    Chocolate Spread and Banana Overnight Oats 31
    Chocolate Truffle Pops 248
    Easy-Peasy Rhubarb Oat Bake 33
    Ginger Snapping Cookies 280
    Mammy's Yummy Porridge with Apple, Berries and
        Seeds 48
    Mammy's Yummy Porridge with Peanut Butter,
        Banana and Nutty Sprinkles 49
    Mammy's Yummy Porridge with Summer Fruits 48
    Nut and Sugar-Free Fruit Granola 34
    Nut-Free Baby Flapjacks 262
    Oat Pancakes with Blueberries 102
    Oatmeal Power Cookies 27
    Overnight Carrot-Cake Oats 105
    Peanut Butter and Jam Overnight Oats 31
    Raspberry Porridge Mini Muffins 36
    Super-Healthy Black Bean Brownies 267
    Super-Healthy Chickpea Cookies 247
olives, Pizza Toasties 77
omelette, Loaded Spanish Omelette with Salad 137
One-Pan Lemon and Garlic Chicken with Asparagus
    and Baby Potatoes 147

onions
    5-Minute Blender Salsa 226
    Baby-Friendly Irish Chowder 145
    Baked Veggie-Loaded Baby Potatoes 189
    Beans, Beans, Good for the Heart Salad 90
    Best Ever Curry-in-a-Hurry Sauce 225
    Breakfast Frittata Mini Muffins 43
    Chicken and Broccoli Pot Pies 166
    Chicken (or Tofu) Tikka Masala 161
    Fajitas with Pulled Beef and Veggies 175
    Granny's Fish and Broccoli Pie 154
    Healthier Pasta Carbonara 128
    Healthy Cauliflower Gratin 206
    Hidden Veggie Pasta Sauce 222
    Home Fries 188
    Italian Quinoa Bites 82
    Loaded Baby Omelette 55
    Moroccan Turkey Meatballs 141
    Patatas Bravas with Chicken/Beans 118
    Pot o' Mussels with Bread for Dipping 136
    Potato and Egg Nests 59
    Potato Rosti 185
    Quinoa Falafels in a Bowl of Yum! 150
    Refried Mexican Black Beans 213
    Salmon and Prawn Linguine 121
    Sticky Chicken Tray Bake 142
    Stuffed Peppers with Sweet Potato Fries 171
    Turkey Burgers and Sweet Potato Fries 178
    Veggie-Loaded Bolognese 152
    Veggie-Loaded Cauliflower Cheese Sauce 223
    Veggie-Loaded Mini Quiches 79
    World's Best Stuffing Balls 216
    Yummy Butter Chicken (or Tofu) 162
    see also red onions; shallots; Spanish onions; spring
        onions
oranges
    Apple Crumble Parfait 41
    Carrot and Apple Salad 202
    Easy-Peasy Rhubarb Oat Bake 33
    Ramen with Sticky Chicken, Beef or Tofu 163
    Sweet Orange Carrots 199
    Sweet Potato Orange Pancakes 64
    Veggie Toasties with Fruit Salad 52
    Overnight Carrot-Cake Oats 105

P

pancakes 61
    Chocolate and Banana Pancakes 62
    Cottage Cheese Pancakes 63
    Oat Pancakes with Blueberries 102
    Quinoa Pancakes 67
    Sweet Potato Orange Pancakes 64
Parmesan cheese
    Baked Pesto Haddock with Garlic Spuds 125

Index

Chicken and Broccoli Pot Pies 166
Healthier Pasta Carbonara 128
Loaded Spanish Omelette with Salad 137
Mammy's Mushy Peas 200
Spinach Gnocchi with Pesto and Veggies 168
Stuffed Peppers with Sweet Potato Fries 171
pasta
Healthier Pasta Carbonara 128
Hidden Veggie Mac and Cheese 177
Kid-Approved Pasta Salad 92
Pesto Pasta with Grilled Veggies and Balsamic
        Tomatoes 117
Salmon and Prawn Linguine 121
Veggie-Loaded Bolognese 152
pastry
Chicken and Broccoli Pot Pies 166
Super-Handy Pies 106
Veggie Pizza Scrolls 101
Veggie-Loaded Mini Quiches 79
Patatas Bravas with Chicken/Beans 118
PBJ Sambo Roll-Ups 111
peaches, Sticky Chicken Tray Bake 142
peanut butter
5-Minute Chocolate Peanut Butter Nice Cream 251
Animal Toasties 72–3
Anytime Rice Squares 287
Bean and Nut Breakfast Bars 39
Chicken on a Stick with Peanut Sauce 85
Chocolate Oaty Cookies 279
Chocolate Truffle Pops 248
Ginger Snapping Cookies 280
Oat-Free Peanut Butter Balls 264
PBJ Sambo Roll-Ups 111
Peanut Butter and Jam Overnight Oats 31
Peanut Butter and Jelly Chocolate Cups 285
Peanut Butter and Sweet Potato Chocolate Mousse
        241
Super-Healthy Chickpea Cookies 247
peas
15-Minute Tex-Mex Wraps 126
Baked Veggie-Loaded Baby Potatoes 189
Bean and Veggie Salad 205
Beans, Beans, Good for the Heart Salad 90
Coconut Poached Salmon with Miso Veggies and
        Rice 133
Granny's Fish and Broccoli Pie 154
Healthier Pasta Carbonara 128
Homemade Fish Goujons with Mushy Peas and
        Oven Chips 172
Kid-Approved Pasta Salad 92
Mammy's Mushy Peas 200
Mango and Lime Quinoa 210
Risotto with Goat's Cheese and Peas 208
Veggie Pizza Scrolls 101

pecan nuts
Apple and Caramel Bites 201
Overnight Carrot-Cake Oats 105
peppers
15-Minute Tex-Mex Wraps 126
Baked Bell Peppers with Eggs 57
Bean and Veggie Bake Bites 215
Bean and Veggie Salad 205
Beans, Beans, Good for the Heart Salad 90
Breakfast Frittata Mini Muffins 43
Chicken and Cheese Quesadillas 81
Chicken on a Stick with Peanut Sauce 85
Chilli con Veggie with the Trimmings 156
Coconut Poached Salmon with Miso Veggies and
        Rice 133
Fajitas with Pulled Beef and Veggies 175
Here Fishy-Fishy Lime, Coriander and Ginger
        Salmon Pops 164
Hidden Veggie Pasta Sauce 222
Hummus, Roasted Veggies, Pittas and Yogurt Dip
        174
Italian Quinoa Bites 82
Kid-Approved Pasta Salad 92
Loaded Baby Omelette 55
Mango and Lime Quinoa 210
Pesto Pasta with Grilled Veggies and Balsamic
        Tomatoes 117
Pizza Toasties 77
Quinoa Falafels in a Bowl of Yum! 150
Ramen with Sticky Chicken, Beef or Tofu 163
Really Quick Rainbow Pizzas 131
Spinach Gnocchi with Pesto and Veggies 168
Sticky Chicken Tray Bake 142
Stuffed Peppers with Sweet Potato Fries 171
Sweet and Sour Chickpea and Noodle Stir-Fry 127
Veggie Pizza Scrolls 101
Veggie Toasties with Fruit Salad 52
Veggie-Loaded Bolognese 152
pesto
Baked Pesto Haddock with Garlic Spuds 125
Easy-Peasy Basil and Spinach Pesto 220
Kid-Approved Pasta Salad 92
Pesto Pasta with Grilled Veggies and Balsamic
        Tomatoes 117
Smashed Avo Eggy Toasties 51
Spinach Gnocchi with Pesto and Veggies 168
pine nuts
Loveliest Bulgur Wheat Salad 209
Pesto Pasta with Grilled Veggies and Balsamic
        Tomatoes 117
pineapples
Brown Bread Ice-Cream Cones 253
Chicken on a Stick with Peanut Sauce 85
Fruit Sticks 260

Kid-Happy Chia Pudding 38
Sweet and Sour Chickpea and Noodle Stir-Fry 127
Veggie Toasties with Fruit Salad 52
pittas, Hummus, Roasted Veggies, Pittas and Yogurt
  Dip 174
pizza
  Pizza Toasties 77
  Really Quick Rainbow Pizzas 131
pomegranates
  Fruit and Veggie Salad with Greek Yogurt and
    Granola 94
  Loveliest Bulgur Wheat Salad 209
Pot o' Mussels with Bread for Dipping 136
potatoes 184
  Asian-Spiced Baby Spuds 186
  Baby-Friendly Irish Chowder 145
  Baked Bell Peppers with Eggs 57
  Baked Veggie-Loaded Baby Potatoes 189
  Granny's Fish and Broccoli Pie 154
  Home Fries 188
  Homemade Fish Goujons with Mushy Peas and
    Oven Chips 172
  Loaded Spanish Omelette with Salad 137
  One-Pan Lemon and Garlic Chicken with Asparagus
    and Baby Potatoes 147
  Patatas Bravas with Chicken/Beans 118
  Potato and Egg Nests 59
  Potato Rosti 185
  Smashed Garlic and Lime Spud Salad 190
  Spinach Gnocchi with Pesto and Veggies 168
  Thai Fishcakes with Potato Squares 122
prawns
  Baby-Friendly Irish Chowder 145
  Salmon and Prawn Linguine 121
protein 9
protein powder, Oat-Free Peanut Butter Balls 264

Q
quesadillas, Chicken and Cheese Quesadillas 81
quiche, Veggie-Loaded Mini Quiches 79
quinoa
  Italian Quinoa Bites 82
  Mango and Lime Quinoa 210
  Quinoa Falafels in a Bowl of Yum! 150
  Quinoa Pancakes 67

R
Rainbow Rocket Pops 261
raisins
  Carrot and Apple Salad 202
  Overnight Carrot-Cake Oats 105
Ramen with Sticky Chicken, Beef or Tofu 163
raspberries
  Chocolate and Banana Pancakes 62
  Cottage Cheese Pancakes 63

Fruit Sticks 260
Mammy's Yummy Porridge with Apple, Berries and
  Seeds 48
Mammy's Yummy Porridge with Summer Fruits 48
Raspberry Porridge Mini Muffins 36
Super-Healthy Banana Splits 255
Xs and Os Waffles with Raspberries and Blueberries
  71
Really Quick Rainbow Pizzas 131
red kidney beans
  Bean and Veggie Bake Bites 215
  Bean and Veggie Salad 205
  Beans, Beans, Good for the Heart Salad 90
  Chilli con Veggie with the Trimmings 156
red onions
  15-Minute Tex-Mex Wraps 126
  Bean and Veggie Salad 205
  Chicken and Cheese Quesadillas 81
  Coconut Poached Salmon with Miso Veggies and
    Rice 133
  Fajitas with Pulled Beef and Veggies 175
  Here Fishy-Fishy Lime, Coriander and Ginger
    Salmon Pops 164
  Hummus, Roasted Veggies, Pittas and Yogurt Dip
    174
  Kid-Approved Pasta Salad 92
  Sticky Chicken Tray Bake 142
  Super-Handy Pies 106
  Sweet and Sour Chickpea and Noodle Stir-Fry 127
  Thai Fishcakes with Potato Squares 122
Refried Mexican Black Beans 213
rhubarb, Easy-Peasy Rhubarb Oat Bake 33
rice
  Chicken (or Tofu) Tikka Masala 161
  Chilli con Veggie with the Trimmings 156
  Coconut Poached Salmon with Miso Veggies and
    Rice 133
  Quinoa Falafels in a Bowl of Yum! 150
  Risotto with Goat's Cheese and Peas 208
  Stuffed Peppers with Sweet Potato Fries 171
  Yummy Butter Chicken (or Tofu) 162
rice, puffed, Anytime Rice Squares 287
Risotto with Goat's Cheese and Peas 208
Roasted Broccoli 198
Roasted Cauliflower with Goat's Cheese 196

S
salads
  Baby Leaves with Fruit Salad 203
  Bean and Veggie Salad 205
  Beans, Beans, Good for the Heart Salad 90
  Carrot and Apple Salad 202
  Fruit and Veggie Salad with Greek Yogurt and
    Granola 94

Index

Kid-Approved Pasta Salad 92
Loveliest Bulgur Wheat Salad 209
salmon
Baby-Friendly Irish Chowder 145
Coconut Poached Salmon with Miso Veggies and Rice 133
Granny's Fish and Broccoli Pie 154
Here Fishy-Fishy Lime, Coriander and Ginger Salmon Pops 164
Salmon and Prawn Linguine 121
salt 19
seeds
Apple Crumble Parfait 41
Baby Leaves with Fruit Salad 203
Bean and Nut Breakfast Bars 39
Easy-Peasy Basil and Spinach Pesto 220
Mammy's Yummy Porridge with Apple, Berries and Seeds 48
Nut and Sugar-Free Fruit Granola 34
Nut-Free Baby Flapjacks 262
Oatmeal Power Cookies 27
Raspberry Porridge Mini Muffins 36
Super-Healthy Black Bean Brownies 267
see also chia seeds; flaxseeds/linseeds; sesame seeds
sesame seeds
Carrot and Apple Salad 202
Nut-Free Baby Flapjacks 262
Ramen with Sticky Chicken, Beef or Tofu 163
shallots
Chilli con Veggie with the Trimmings 156
Risotto with Goat's Cheese and Peas 208
Sweet Potato and Carrot Curried Hummus with 10-Minute Falafels 78
Veggie-Loaded Mini Muffins 96
Smashed Avo Eggy Toasties 51
Smashed Garlic and Lime Spud Salad 190
soy sauce
Chicken on a Stick with Peanut Sauce 85
Coconut Poached Salmon with Miso Veggies and Rice 133
Ramen with Sticky Chicken, Beef or Tofu 163
Sweet Orange Carrots 199
Sweet and Sour Chickpea and Noodle Stir-Fry 127
Spanish onions
Bean and Veggie Bake Bites 215
Chilli con Veggie with the Trimmings 156
Loaded Spanish Omelette with Salad 137
spinach
10-Minute Chickpea Burgers 130
Baked Bell Peppers with Eggs 57
Baked Pesto Haddock with Garlic Spuds 125
Breakfast Frittata Mini Muffins 43
Chicken and Broccoli Pot Pies 166
Easy-Peasy Basil and Spinach Pesto 220
Hidden Veggie Pasta Sauce 222

Potato and Egg Nests 59
Rainbow Rocket Pops 261
Spinach Gnocchi with Pesto and Veggies 168
Sweet Potato Grow-Quettes 193
Veggie Pizza Scrolls 101
Veggie Toasties with Fruit Salad 52
spirulina, Healthy Rainbow Sprinkles 257
spring onions
10-Minute Chickpea Burgers 130
Baby Leaves with Fruit Salad 203
Mango and Lime Quinoa 210
Ramen with Sticky Chicken, Beef or Tofu 163
sprinkles, Healthy Rainbow Sprinkles 257
Sticky Chicken Tray Bake 142
strawberries
Animal Toasties 72–3
Baby Leaves with Fruit Salad 203
Chocolate and Banana Pancakes 62
Fruit Sticks 260
Healthy Strawberry Blondies 239
Mammy's Yummy Porridge with Summer Fruits 48
Strawberry Jam 234–5
Super-Healthy Banana Splits 255
Stuffed Peppers with Sweet Potato Fries 171
Sugar-Free Chocolate Chunky Mini Muffins 277
Super-Handy Pies 106
Super-Healthy Banana Splits 255
Super-Healthy Black Bean Brownies 267
Super-Healthy Chickpea Cookies 247
Super-Yummy Baby Doughnuts 272
Sweet Orange Carrots 199
sweet potatoes
Baby-Friendly Veggie Fritters 87
Chicken Tenders with Roasted Veggies 151
Here Fishy-Fishy Lime, Coriander and Ginger Salmon Pops 164
Peanut Butter and Sweet Potato Chocolate Mousse 241
Sticky Chicken Tray Bake 142
Stuffed Peppers with Sweet Potato Fries 171
Sweet Potato and Carrot Curried Hummus with 10-Minute Falafels 78
Sweet Potato and Carrot Superhero Muffins 95
Sweet Potato and Cauliflower Cakes 86
Sweet Potato Fries with 2-Minute Garlic Dip 194
Sweet Potato Grow-Quettes 193
Sweet Potato Orange Pancakes 64
Turkey Burgers and Sweet Potato Fries 178
Sweet and Sour Chickpea and Noodle Stir-Fry 127
sweetcorn
15-Minute Tex-Mex Wraps 126
Bean and Veggie Bake Bites 215
Bean and Veggie Salad 205
Really Quick Rainbow Pizzas 131
Veggie Pizza Scrolls 101

T
tacos, Fajitas with Pulled Beef and Veggies 175
tahini
  Baby-Friendly Curried Hummus 229
  Best Ever Curry-in-a-Hurry Sauce 225
  Chicken on a Stick with Peanut Sauce 85
  Chocolate Truffle Pops 248
  Hummus, Roasted Veggies, Pittas and Yogurt Dip 174
  Quinoa Falafels in a Bowl of Yum! 150
  Sweet Potato and Carrot Curried Hummus with 10-Minute Falafels 78
  Tahini Dressing 150
Thai Fishcakes with Potato Squares 122
Toddler-and-Kid-Approved Banana and Walnut Muffins 98
tofu
  Chicken (or Tofu) Tikka Masala 161
  Ramen with Sticky Chicken, Beef or Tofu 163
  Yummy Chicken (or Tofu) Butter Chicken 162
tomatoes/tomato purée
  15-Minute Tex-Mex Wraps 126
  3-Ingredient Pizza Sauce 230
  Best Ever Curry-in-a-Hurry Sauce 225
  Chicken and Cheese Quesadillas 81
  Chicken (or Tofu) Tikka Masala 161
  Chilli con Veggie with the Trimmings 156
  Fajitas with Pulled Beef and Veggies 175
  Hidden Veggie Pasta Sauce 222
  Italian Quinoa Bites 82
  Moroccan Turkey Meatballs 141
  Patatas Bravas with Chicken/Beans 118
  Pizza Toasties 77
  Pot o' Mussels with Bread for Dipping 136
  Stuffed Peppers with Sweet Potato Fries 171
  Super-Handy Pies 106
  Veggie Pizza Scrolls 101
  Veggie-Loaded Bolognese 152
  Yummy Butter Chicken (or Tofu) 162
  see also cherry tomatoes
tortillas
  15-Minute Tex-Mex Wraps 126
  Chicken and Cheese Quesadillas 81
  Really Quick Rainbow Pizzas 131
turkey
  Moroccan Turkey Meatballs 141
  Turkey Burgers and Sweet Potato Fries 178

V
vegans 15
vegetarians 9–10
Veggie Pizza Scrolls 101
Veggie Toasties with Fruit Salad 52
Veggie-Loaded Bolognese 152

Veggie-Loaded Cauliflower Cheese Sauce 223
Veggie-Loaded Mini Muffins 96
Veggie-Loaded Mini Quiches 79

W
waffles
  Waffles and Chocolate Nice Cream 68
  Xs and Os Waffles with Raspberries and Blueberries 71
Weekly Meal Planner 202–3
Whatever's in the Fridge Dinner 174
World's Best Stuffing Balls 216
wraps
  15-Minute Tex-Mex Wraps 126
  Chicken and Cheese Quesadillas 81

X
Xs and Os Waffles with Raspberries and Blueberries 71

Y
yogurt
  Chicken and Broccoli Pot Pies 166
  Fruit Sticks 260
  Quinoa Pancakes 67
  Salmon and Prawn Linguine 121
  Yummy Chicken (or Tofu) Butter Chicken 162
  see also Greek yogurt
Yummy Chicken (or Tofu) Butter Chicken 162

Z
Zingy Mango Mousse 258